The Key To Contentment and Happiness

The Key To

CONTENTMENT

and

HAPPINESS

*A collection of quotes, correspondence
and commentary*

J. Taylor Starkey, M.D.
AUTHOR/EDITOR

© Copyright © 1996 by J. Taylor Starkey, M.D.
All rights reserved.

No part of this book may be reproduced or transmitted in any form or by any means, electronic or mechanical—including photocopying, recording, or by any information storage or retrieval system—without written permission from the Author, except for the inclusion of brief quotations in a review.

Credit for any quotations not already within the public domain is hereby specifically acknowledged as resting with the individual authors, if known.

ISBN 0-9652391-0-1

For information or to order additional copies of this book, contact:
Diversion Publishing of Texas
404 W. Guadalupe
Victoria, Texas 77901

Published in the United States of America
Burke Publishing Company
San Antonio, Texas

Many thanks to my wife, **Myra,** for her emotional and
technical support on this project . . .

To my children, **Miles, Hannah,** and **Spencer,**
who afforded me the peace and quiet
to complete this task . . .

And finally, to **Dr. Rex Kirkley,**
who helped me re-establish the balance
in my life and medical practice.
Dr. Kirkley was a fine old family physician,
a friend, counselor, and kindred spirit of mine
who passed away in February 1996.
To him I dedicate this book.

Personal Correspondence By

Tom Landry	Naomi Judd
Jack Canfield	Mary Kay Ash
Dr. Hanoch McCarty	Governor Edwin Edwards
Dave Barry	Congressman Henry B. Gonzales
Maury Povich	Vanna White
Art Linkletter	Senator Phil Gramm
Tim Allen	Oliver North
Susan Ungaro	Dan Rather
Robert W. Reasoner	Floyd Shilanski
Senator Robert Kerrey	Glenn McIntyre
D. Trinidad Hunt	Erik Olesen
Governor Kirk Fordice	Dr. Eric Anderson
Florence Littauer	Nido Qubein
Joe Scruggs	Alan Cohen
Senator John Ashcroft	Governor Lincoln Almond
Patricia Lorenz	Bettie B. Youngs
Michael Maudlin	Patricia Fripp
Dr. Glen Griffin	Harold Myra
Governor Frank Keating	Dr. Harold Bloomfield
Steve Farrar	Mike Buettell
Dan Bolin	Governor Thomas R. Carper
Glenna Salsbury	Stan Dale
Senator Charles Grassley	Ben Burton

Dr. Michael J. Murphy	Governor Tommy Thompson
Dennis Mannering	W. Mitchell
Rick Gelinas	Congressman Henry Waxman
Larry Winget	Buck Owens
Dottie Walters	Congressman Charles Rangel
Governor George Bush	Governor Bob Miller
Dan Clark	Joe Batten
Ralph Archbold	Gary Moses
Burt Dubin	Wayne Watkins
Helen Gurley Brown	Governor George Allen
Bobbie Gee	Herbert H. Reynolds
Dr. Joseph Hance	Timothy Fults
Mark Victor Hansen	Helice Bridges
Russ Matthews	Sandra Williams
Robert L. Bartley	Gaylan Duncan
Howard Hendricks	John Swoboda
Hara Estroff Marano	David Barnhart
Congressman Craig Thomas	Sharon Steen
David E. Davis	Mayor Marion Barry
Jim Wright	Dr. Joyce Brothers
Dr. Tom Renshaw	Daniel Zellmer
Governor Brereton Jones	John O'Sullivan
D. Gyllensvard	Rex Kirkley M.D.
Melba Coleman	Tony Luna
Jeep Collins	Bill Glass
Governor Benjamin Nelson	

Introduction

What is the key to happiness, contentment, or fulfillment in life?

I first believed that this question was exclusively in the realm of those suffering mid-life crisis. It isn't something that young children or even teenagers often contemplate. They certainly know the difference between happiness and sadness, content and discontent, but they are usually too busy playing, imagining in fantasy, going to school, or thinking about the opposite sex to engage is such deep thought. Young adults in their twenties are generally occupied with finishing their education, adjusting to marriage, starting families, and becoming established in their careers or occupations. Often there is still too much outward activity to allow time to be introspective. Only those who suffer some sort of major failure in the process may start to ponder the purpose of life. A death of a close parent, a storybook marriage that turns sour and ends in divorce, or an unsuccessful attempt to achieve a desired career, may leave the disheartened individual wondering if happiness exists.

The dust finally settles for most during their thirties or forties. For those able to easily slow down, they give a sigh of relief, and relax. For others who are caught in a rat race that

→ THE KEY TO CONTENTMENT AND HAPPINESS ←

won't let them off, they often throw up the white flag of surrender and jump off. In either situation, amidst all the activity, an uneasiness may start to creep into one's life. What is the purpose of life? What has meaning? What brings real happiness, contentment, or fulfillment? One would want to know so they could plan their future course of action. Surely some deliberate effort is required.

It seems that in middle age and later, the greatest trigger to the big question is a failure of one of our major personal goals or projects. We seem to react to significant disappointments or rejections by feeling, "If that wasn't my purpose in life then what is?" Or even if some major goal is achieved without experiencing the anticipated contentment or fulfillment we think, "If that didn't give me joy then what will?"

Age grants us no immunity. I recently had a heart to heart talk with my 92 year old grandmother. She moves a lot slower these days but her mind is still sharp. She lives in a nice nursing home and because of its security, numerous fellow residents for companionship, and abundant activities, she seems to like it more than she is willing to admit. She appeared melancholy and I asked why. She fought back tears and said that life just hadn't turned out the way she had expected. As I grew up around her she had always seemed content and happy. She stayed busy taking care of my grandfather when she wasn't entertaining or feeding us. She was a real servant and enjoyable to be around. And now she lacked fulfillment.

I had so hoped that the question of mid-life could be answered, that the key to contentment could be found, and then never dealt with again. I suppose the quest is ongoing. The solutions change.

This book contains quotations, opinions from the correspondence of the many contributors, and personal observation. I wrote letters to people all across the United States and asked them, "What is the key to contentment, fulfillment, or happiness is life?" This note was sent to Senators, Congress-

THE KEY TO CONTENTMENT AND HAPPINESS

men, Governors, authors, journalists, speakers, editors, ministers, physicians, business leaders, personalities, and individuals from all walks of life, some famous and some obscure. Many chose not to answer, either due to lack of time or perhaps more likely as a simple result of having no clear thought on the matter. A good number did respond and their replies were uplifting and interesting. It became a joy each day to open the mail. I'm glad they chose to share.

I found it interesting that when I would tell people about this project, their response was always the same. "So what is the key to contentment and happiness?" they would ask. I could only smile and say that I knew what it was for me but I didn't know what the key was for them.

I hope in this book you will find answers that speak to you. There is no one solution for everyone as each of our lives are different, so it can be a lonely search. We are all individual creations, each with unique life experiences that color us and vary our perception of the world. Good luck. Your answer is out there. It may be closer that you think.

— **J. Taylor Starkey M.D.**

The Key To
CONTENTMENT
and
HAPPINESS

❧ THE KEY TO CONTENTMENT AND HAPPINESS ❦

PHOTO BY LUCILLE GERALD

THE KEY TO CONTENTMENT AND HAPPINESS

The search for happiness is one of the chief sources of unhappiness.

Eric Hoffer (1902-1983)

I think the key to contentment, fulfillment or happiness in life is to work your brains out! Work has always been my chloroform ... When one is working, one can't think too intensely about personal problems, insecurity, lack of great looks or lots of other trivia! The harder you work, the more you get paid and the more you get appreciated and that takes care of lots of life's problems. Is one a workaholic? Yes ... remorselessly, contentedly and guiltlessly!

Helen Gurley Brown, *Editor, Cosmopolitan Magazine*

The essence of philosophy is that a man should so live that his happiness shall depend as little as possible on external things.

Epictetus (ca. A.D. 90)

Happiness is having a large, loving, caring, close-knit family in another city.

George Burns

The key to happiness and contentment in life is not a quick fix, but rather the result of long term investments in those we love and care about—namely, nourishing our soul, a happy and respectful connection to family and friends, productive and meaningful work, and building safe and connected communities.

Bettie B. Youngs, Ph.D., *Author, Speaker, Consultant*

THE KEY TO CONTENTMENT AND HAPPINESS

The great essentials of happiness are something to do, something to love, and something to hope for.

Anonymous

I believe contentment, fulfillment, and happiness are synonyms for "Inner Peace." To achieve total peace, our daily activities must reflect our core values. If the things we think about are different than the things we do, we will never be happy!

Dan Clark, *Motivational Speaker*

Happiness and Beauty are by-products.

George Bernard Shaw (1856-1950)

Lord of himself, though not of lands;
And having nothing, yet hath all.
How happy is he born and taught,
That serveth not another's will;
Whose armor is his honest thought,
And simple truth his utmost skill!

Sir Henry Wotton (1568-1639)

The key to contentment and happiness?—
Follow your heart . . . It never lies!

Vanna White, *TV Personality*

The secret of happiness is not in doing what you like, but in liking what you do.

Anonymous

Make one person happy each day . . . even if it's yourself.

Anonymous

THE KEY TO CONTENTMENT AND HAPPINESS

Happiness is a butterfly . . . the more you chase it, the more it flies away from you and hides. But stop chasing it, put away your net and busy yourself with other, more productive things than the pursuit of happiness, and it will sneak up on you from behind and perch on your shoulder.

Rabbi Harold Kushner,
from WHEN ALL YOU'VE EVER WANTED ISN'T ENOUGH

After interviewing hundreds of rich and famous people, it is clear to me that money and fame don't automatically make people happy. It has to come from within. I'd rather have a million smiles in my heart than a million dollars in my pocket.

Robin Leach, *Author & TV Personality*

Happiness comes from doing good for others for as Ben Franklin said, "The Noblest Question in the world is what good may I do in it?"

Ralph Archbold, *Speaker*

To be without some of the things you want is an indispensable part of happiness.

Anonymous

Happiness is a perpetual possession of being well deceived . . . the serene and peaceful state of being a fool among knaves or scoundrels.
Little wealth, much health, and a life by stealth.

Jonathan Swift (1667-1745)

There is only one way to happiness and that is to cease worrying about things which are beyond the power of our will.

Epictetus (ca. 90 A.D.)

↠ THE KEY TO CONTENTMENT AND HAPPINESS ↞

PHOTO BY ROGER KURTNER

→ THE KEY TO CONTENTMENT AND HAPPINESS ←

The wise man is happy when he gains his own approbation and the fool when he recommends himself to the applause of those about him.

Joseph Addison (1672-1719)

I believe that contentment, happiness, and fulfillment is not a destination; it is a journey. If you don't like what you are doing on the way through your life, whatever success you have near the end of it is not truly success (i.e. happiness, contentment, etc.). Do what you like to do, and continue to do it, and it should be something you can do best without worrying about the reward. You will do a better job, spend more time at it, and eventually your success will be sweeter. "Work hard!" cannot be over-stressed. Hard work is more important than talent or brains, because without hard work, talent and brains are wasted. I personally have worked hard all my life and I am just as busy today as I have ever been, and am enjoying life ever more as the years go by.

I believe firmly in educating oneself, and it is an ongoing process, not "finished" at the college campus. All of life is an education and I am thankful and happy that this is so. Curiosity may kill cats, but without it humankind is straight-jacketed; curiosity and imagination go hand in hand.

Finally, play fair with the people around you. Your reputation and character are part of the march towards happiness, contentment, and fulfillment.

Art Linkletter, *TV Personality, Author*

What happiness the rural maid attends,
In cheerful labour while each day she spends!
She gratefully receives what Heav'n has sent,
And rich in poverty, enjoys content.

John Gay (1685-1732), *from RURAL SPORTS*

THE KEY TO CONTENTMENT AND HAPPINESS

Don't put the search for happiness first in your life. Put happiness at least second, and maybe a good bit lower, on your scale of values, desires, and needs. The reason is simple. We don't get happiness when we seek it as our number one goal. Happiness always eludes us when we make it first on our list of priorities.

Dr. Ross West, *Author, Speaker*

People are about as happy as they make up their minds to be.

Abraham Lincoln (1809-1865)

About ninety percent of the things in our lives are right and about ten percent are wrong. If we want to be happy, all we have to do is concentrate on the ninety percent that are right and ignore the ten percent that are wrong. If we want to be worried and bitter and have stomach ulcers, all we have to do is concentrate on the ten percent that are wrong and ignore the ninety percent that are glorious.

Dale Carnegie (1888-1955)

In my life it is my family that provides the most contentment and my belief of the Supreme Being. I have chosen a profession, where when I can help someone, it gives me a sincere reward. Just today I had a two hour meeting with a couple that will probably be losing their daughter to anorexia. They needed some place to cry and hurt and discuss the things you don't want to talk about, such as planning for the continuation of life after their teenager. I think it is my family and the warm feelings of touching people that is my key to contentment, fulfillment, and happiness in life.

Floyd Shilanski, *Author, Speaker, Financial Planner*

THE KEY TO CONTENTMENT AND HAPPINESS

The rays of happiness, like those of light, are colorless when unbroken.

Henry Wadsworth Longfellow (1807-1882)

The spider's most attenuated thread
Is cord, is cable, to man's tender tie
On earthly bliss; it breaks at every breeze.

Edward Young (1683-1765), *from* N*ight* T*houghts*

I find contentment or fulfillment demonstrated daily by those patients who have discovered the answer for themselves.

It's not the classic triumvirate of power, money, and sex. The key seems to be a composite of having a sense of humor and not taking one's self too seriously; of having integrity enough to permit looking in a mirror without flinching—but without preening; of being needed and being able to answer that need; and, above all, of going through life's journey with a person you love more than very life itself.

Eric Anderson, M.D., *Physician, Journalist*

Love is the key to contentment and happiness.

Erik Olesen, *Speaker, Author of* M*astering the* W*inds of* C*hange*

The key to happiness in life, is having the time and means to live life, as well as having a loved one and good health, to enjoy life.

Glen McIntyre, *Motivational Speaker*

All who would win joy must share it; happiness was born a twin.

Lord Byron (1788-1824)

❧ THE KEY TO CONTENTMENT AND HAPPINESS ❦

PHOTO BY TAYLOR STARKEY

THE KEY TO CONTENTMENT AND HAPPINESS

The longing of the heart—unrevealed and deep—leads to dreams. These dreams float as time passes, refusing to be sunk by the anchors of hindrance and hardship. They grow into possibilities kept alive by hope and determination. Vague possibilities lead to concrete opportunities that stir up the soul with gratifying, satisfying stimulation . . . which ultimately becomes actual accomplishment, the ace trump of fulfillment.

Chuck Swindoll, *from Seasons of Change*

Happiness is probably the easiest emotion to feel, the most elusive to create deliberately, and the most difficult to define. It is experienced differently by different people.

Norman Cousins, *Author, Former Editor of Saturday Review*

There can be no happiness if the things we believe in are different from the things we do.

Anonymous

My four-year-old son Spencer and I were piddling around in the garage at our weekend home. We had gotten out of town for a guys-only weekend. We had been doing some male bonding activities such as roasting weenies and marshmallows on an open fire, exploring out in the field behind the house, and making Indian bowls and animals from clay we dug out of the ditch.

Spencer looked at me sweetly and said, "If I ask you for anything in this garage would you give it to me?"

"Well . . . yes, I suppose so, "I replied, "Everything I have is yours. Everything I work for is for my children."

I could not imagine what he wanted. Was it my old ten speed bike? Did he want to push the lawn mower? Could he be wanting to drive the car? Is it possible he wanted possession of the garage itself for a clubhouse? He just stood there and looked at me while I looked back at him.

"So what do you want?" I finally asked.

THE KEY TO CONTENTMENT AND HAPPINESS

"A nail," he said.

Simply a nail— I handed him a nail from one of the many sacks of nails on the shelf. He examined it briefly, saw that it was indeed a nail, and ambled off contentedly.

It seems that much of the unhappiness and discontent that adults have is a result of their loss of an appreciation for the simple things in life. A kid finds enjoyment in a nail, a rope swing in a tree, a big black bug he found in the yard, a stick that he pretends is a gun, digging in the dirt, or playing with the water hose. Adults are concerned with bigger houses, better cars, nicer landscaping, perfecting their golf game, being in the right clubs, and wearing the right clothes. Kids don't naturally take much notice to all of that. Dissatisfaction seems to be something they learn from peers, parents, and television.

Kids prefer what is simple. If you don't believe it then observe their eating habits. If you serve them some food that is basically brown with little green things in it like herbs, chives, or sweet peppers they will automatically pick them out before even daring to taste it. If you fix a dish of green colored food with brown things in it then they remove the brown things. They don't like to eat multicolored items. My wife was sitting on the couch recently with my young son. She was reading *Bon Appetit* and concentrating on a new gourmet recipe. He was looking at the pictures in a family/women's magazine and occasionally glancing suspiciously at the unusual food pictures in her magazine. Finally, he ran across an ad in his with a photo of a dinner of macaroni and cheese and fried chicken. "Look, mom," he said excitedly as he shoved the magazine in front of her, "Here's some good food!"

We would do well to rediscover the joys of the simple things in life. Our kids might welcome a new playmate. I think I'll go get a spoon from the silverware drawer, go out in the yard and see if my kids could use an assistant digger. Maybe my wife could cook us some corn dogs for lunch.

J. Taylor Starkey

THE KEY TO CONTENTMENT AND HAPPINESS

He is happy that knoweth not himself to be otherwise.

Thomas Fuller (1654-1734)

There is that in me—I do not know what it is—
but I know it is in me . . .
I do not know it—it is without name—it is a word unsaid;
It is not in any dictionary, utterance, symbol.
Something it swings on more than the earth I swing on.
To it the creation is the friend whose embracing awakes me . . .
It is not chaos or death—it is form, union, plan,
it is eternal life—it is Happiness.

Walt Whitman (1819-1892)

The secret of contentment is the discovery by every man of his own powers and limitations, finding satisfaction in a line of activity which he can do well, plus the wisdom to know that his place, no matter how important or successful he is, never counts very much in the universe.

Lin Yutang (1895-1976)

Cheerfulness keeps up a kind of daylight in the mind, and fills it with a steady and perpetual serenity.

Joseph Addison (1672-1719)

It is not how much we have, but how much we enjoy, that makes happiness.

Charles Haddon Spurgeon (1834-1892)

Happiness and fulfillment comes from seeing the light in a child's eyes; knowing that they "got it." Contentment comes from knowing you caused it to happen.

Melba Coleman, *Teacher and mom*

❖ THE KEY TO CONTENTMENT AND HAPPINESS ❖

PHOTO BY TAYLOR STARKEY

THE KEY TO CONTENTMENT AND HAPPINESS

The question, "What is the key to contentment, fulfillment, or happiness in life?" is a truly personal one. I cannot presume to speak for others or provide a definitive answer. But for myself, the question reminds me of my Aunt Guadalupe's missal I once read as a youngster. The words were of Santa Teresa de Jesus, and it seemed to be a heavenly message:

> Let nothing trouble you.
> Let nothing frighten you.
> All things pass away.
> God only is immutable.
> Patience overcomes all difficulties.
> Those who possess God want nothing.
> God alone suffices.

These words gave me the courage that was essential to self-respect. From then on, fear did not overwhelm me. And because of this I have been able to confront the challenges of my lifetime with self-respect, integrity and passion. Life has been a long road for me, with many twists and turns, and even a little trail-blazing at times. Without self-respect and love of oneself in a true biblical sense, fulfillment and contentment in life only give way to folly.

Henry B. Gonzalez, *U.S. Congressman*

The key to happiness or contentment is truly knowing what you need and having the ability to love others. This happens through intentional spiritual and emotional growth and by God's grace, which sets us free to grow.

Daniel Zellmer, *Lutheran Minister*

Contentment comes through losing one's self in helping others through community and charitable causes and, in the process, discovering so much about our own sense of behavioral understanding.

Dr. Nido Qubein, *Speaker, Management Consultant*

THE KEY TO CONTENTMENT AND HAPPINESS

The love for and from one's family is unquestionably the key to a truly successful life.
Lincoln Almond, *Governor of Rhode Island*

Love is where we come from, who we are, and where we are going.
Alan Cohen, *Speaker, Author*

For a person who is working, there are three things that are important for contentment. They are career, community, and compensation—in that order. First of all, you must enjoy your job. You have to like what you are doing. Second, you should enjoy your community. If you are living in a bad, unpleasant environment then your family will be very unhappy and so will you during your time off. Lastly comes the compensation. If you like your job and where you live, making a lot of money isn't important! You just need to make enough to meet your needs.
Tom Renshaw, M.D., *Orthopedics Department Chairman, University of South Carolina Medical School*

Happiness is not an accident. Nor is it something you wish for. Happiness is something you design.

The walls we build around us to keep out the sadness also keep out the joy.

Jim Rohn, *Motivational Speaker, Author*

Let him who would be happy for a day, go to the barber; for a week marry a wife; for a month, buy him a new horse; for a year, build him a new house; for all his life time, be an honest man.
Thomas Fuller (1608-1661), *from WORTHIES*

→ THE KEY TO CONTENTMENT AND HAPPINESS ←

There once was a poor Jewish farmer who lived in a small hut with his wife, three kids, and their dog. He worked hard in his rocky fields, often from dawn to dusk, just to raise enough crops to feed his family and have enough left over to barter for their basic needs. One rainy day as he sat in his hut, he began to think and realized that he was not really happy. This concerned him so much that he went to talk to his rabbi. The farmer told the rabbi about his life and his discontent. The rabbi instructed him to go home and bring his goat inside the hut with him and his wife, kids, and dog and then to return in one week for a visit. The farmer did just that and returned to the rabbi a week later. He was still unhappy, so the rabbi told him to go back and bring his chickens in his hut to live with him, his wife, kids, dog, and goat, and to come back in a week. He did just that and a week later returned, still melancholy. The rabbi sent him home telling him now to bring in the cow to stay in the hut with him, his wife, the kids, dog, goat, and chickens. After a week he returned to the rabbi expressing great frustration and worsening sadness. The rabbi told him to go home and put the cow outside. The farmer felt some relief and went home. The next week he was still fairly unhappy so the rabbi told him to place the chickens back in the yard. He was starting to feel more content. A week later, after the rabbi allowed him to put the goat back outside, it was again just his wife, kids, and dog. He returned to the rabbi one last time to tell him that he was now happy.

Jewish Folk Tale

The key to contentment is to
know thyself—
don't over project—
stay focused.

Joseph Hance, M.D., *Family Physician*

THE KEY TO CONTENTMENT AND HAPPINESS

PHOTO BY TAYLOR STARKEY

THE KEY TO CONTENTMENT AND HAPPINESS

I'm not certain that there is a universal key to unlock the door to contentment, fulfillment, and happiness, in fact, I am convinced that each of us has to find his own way. For myself, I've never gone wrong when I tried to follow the single best piece of advice I ever got. It came from my Mother, who told me as a child to work hard, always try to do what is right and the rest will take care of itself.

Phil Gramm, *U.S. Senator*

Happiness is not found in self-contemplation; it is perceived only when it is reflected from another.

Samuel Johnson (1709-1784)

Each age, like every individual, has its own characteristic intoxication; we must seek in each decade the joys natural to our years. If play is the effervescence of childhood, and love is the wine of youth, the solace of age is understanding. If you would be content in age, be wise and learn something everyday. Education is not a task, it is a life long happiness, an ennobling intimacy with great men, and unhurried excursion into all realms of loveliness and wisdom. If in youth we fell in love with beauty, in maturity we can make friends with genius.

Will Durant (1885-1981)

The door to happiness is outward.

Anonymous

A man's happiness is to do a man's true work.

Marcus Aurelius (121-180 A.D.), *Roman Emperor*

THE KEY TO CONTENTMENT AND HAPPINESS

What is the key to contentment, fulfillment or happiness you ask? I am a searcher for this answer myself, therefore I do not know it yet. However, I am convinced that it has much to do with the direction in which we direct our concerns and our growth:

Inward = Discontent, Failure, Stagnation
Outward = Contentment, Fulfillment, Happiness

Ben Burton, *Speaker, Writer, Humorist*

One great and common method of achieving happiness is to not think too much. Some of the most troubled souls are those who are contemplative, philosophical or theological sorts. Not to say that philosophy and theology are not important and worthwhile pursuits, only that those involved in the deep thought often overvalue their personal revelations in the grand scheme of things. That person's great burden is in thinking that if they don't clearly express their almost divinely inspired truths, mankind may forever lose these unique thoughts. Something on the level of Beethoven's Fifth Symphony or Shakespeare's *Hamlet*. To think that humanity's advancement may rest on one's philosophical, political, or theological opinions, understandings or discoveries is an awesome and overpowering responsibility!

Life certainly has no easy answers. In fact, often the deeper we search, the more questions we find. That can be very frustrating. We sometimes overload our brain trying to answer questions that most people never ask.

There are many content, common laborers who simply work hard all day, spend the appropriate time with the wife and kids, play catch with their mutt in the backyard, go bowling three nights a week, drink cheap beer regularly, belch more that average, and sleep well every night. And they don't worry much about life.

J. Taylor Starkey

THE KEY TO CONTENTMENT AND HAPPINESS

We have no right to consume happiness without producing it than to consume wealth without producing it.

George Bernard Shaw (1856-1950)

A man should always consider how much he has, more than how much he wants, and how much more unhappy he might be than he really is.

Joseph Addison (1672-1719)

Wayne Gretzky has scored more goals than any other player in professional hockey and he has become something of a shrine in that sport. Asked how he scores so many times, he replied, "It's really quite simple. I go to where the puck is going to be, not where it is." To be successful in anything, one must go to where the puck is going to be, not to where it is. And never chase it!

Rick Gelinas, *Motivational Speaker*

The laws of the cosmos seem to be as little concerned about human happiness as the laws of the United States are concerned about human decency. Whoever set them in motion apparently had something quite different in mind, something that we cannot even guess at.

H. L. Mencken (1880-1956)

Religion is the opiate of the masses.
The first requisite for the happiness of the people is the abolition of religion.

Karl Marx (1818-1883)

For contentment: Put your trust in Jesus Christ.

Chuck Grassley, *U.S. Senator*

❖ THE KEY TO CONTENTMENT AND HAPPINESS ❖

PHOTO BY JAMES WILCOX

THE KEY TO CONTENTMENT AND HAPPINESS

> The key to contentment in life is to develop a personal relationship with Christ who created us for this purpose.
>
> **Glenna Salsbury, *Motivational Speaker***

Many people seek their contentment and happiness through spirituality. When I posed the "key to contentment" question to various individuals, a good number said that it was Jesus Christ, or God, or through achieving a higher plane of consciousness, or finding the light within yourself. These folks had come to the realization that contentment was not to be had from worldly, natural, material things and therefore it must be supernatural or spiritual.

Obviously different people have different spiritual guides and each individual, if they have mentally invested themselves in their beliefs, would be fairly dogmatic in their convictions. Many of those who claim to be spiritual seem peaceful and content but unfortunately there are an equal number who appear unsettled, unhappy, and still searching for answers.

As a Christian, I undoubtedly view the world from that perspective. And as much as I would like to claim that if one would accept Christ and his teachings, then true happiness and contentment would follow, my personal experience and observation of fellow Christians doesn't confirm that. When a fellow believer tells me that Jesus Christ is the key to contentment I say—Why? Be more specific. What exactly is it about Christ that takes away your cares, troubles, discontent and stress? Is it that you are certain you are on the right path and following the one true way? Is it that you have all the answers? Is it the comfort that there is a greater power in ultimate control? Are you becoming increasingly more at peace? Does your religious experience involve a warm, loving relationship or is it just some dry, ancient list of do's and don'ts that you feel compelled to follow at the urging of your conscience? These same queries could be posed to anyone regarding their spiritual belief system.

THE KEY TO CONTENTMENT AND HAPPINESS

One method for achieving total contentment through religion is to so deeply immerse ourselves in spiritual study and concentration that we shut out the rest of the world. Only by secluding ourselves in a monastery, possibly our homes, or sometimes in the right part of town can we ignore the hate, poverty, crime and selfishness of the world. But we should feel compelled to go out into the world and push back this darkness. We can't fix the problems of society although we can each make a positive difference in our small way. And through the good we create and nurture, happiness will come for ourselves and those we impact.

Some people who claim to be spiritual are not content and happy because they are still so entangled and burdened by their worldly material ways. Many don't follow Biblical direction. By critical observation it would appear that the actions being taught would definitely make for a better life than doing the opposite. This is true whether an individual believes in God or not. The Bible teaches us that we should love our neighbor as ourself and repeatedly instructs us to be loving and sharing and not selfish. The converse course of action would be the law of the jungle—the survival of the fittest—put yourself first—don't let anybody get in the way of your desires. The scriptures tell us to take care of our bodies, to enjoy life in moderation, and to be totally faithful to our spouses. The opposite would be to seek maximum pleasure and euphoria regardless of the adverse health effects, to ignore our relationship commitments and to seek "love" with whomever we feel the attraction or desire. The Bible says to seek after the spiritual and to store our treasures in heaven. The contrary would be sell our souls to acquire the maximum material goods and assets. It seems sensible and logical to strive to follow the biblical guidelines. To do otherwise would most certainly cause problems either acutely or over the long term.

As a physician, I occasionally am involved in intimate and personal discussions with my patients. We talk of events in

THE KEY TO CONTENTMENT AND HAPPINESS

their lives that have stressed them in some way. I have never had anyone come to me and say, "Doc, I feel great. I went out last night with the boys, drank 18 beers, swigged down I don't know how many Tequila shots, smoked four cigars, and stayed up until two in the morning. I just feel fantastic today. I think I'll start doing that every night!" Nor have I ever had anyone come in and say, "Doctor, let me tell you what I did. I have been sneaking around on my wife and had an affair with my secretary. You know she's married too and has a couple of kids. Anyway, my wife found out so I had to give it up. But I had a super time. It couldn't have turned out better. I can't believe I waited so long to get into this adultery business. I can hardly wait to do it again!"

So can spirituality lead to contentment and happiness? It at least offers more hope than the opposite path. Religion, or any other activity or endeavor for that matter, can never be without problems as long as it is practiced by imperfect humans. We can only strive to do our best.

J. Taylor Starkey

Happiness is the only sanction of life; where happiness fails, existence remains a mad and lamentable experiment.

George Santayana (1863-1952)

The true felicity of life is to be free from anxieties and the things that upset us, to understand and do our duties to God and man, and to enjoy the present without any serious dependence on the future.

Lucius Seneca (4 B.C.-65 A.D.)

Whoever does not regard what he has as most ample wealth, is unhappy, though he be master of the world.

Epicurus (342-270 B.C.)

❧ THE KEY TO CONTENTMENT AND HAPPINESS ❦

PHOTO BY JAMES WILCOX

THE KEY TO CONTENTMENT AND HAPPINESS

God made us: invented us as a man invents an engine. A car is made to run on gasoline, and it would not run properly on anything else. Now God designed the human machine to run on Himself. He Himself is the fuel our spirits were designed to burn, or the food our spirits were designed to feed on. There is no other. That is why it is just no good asking God to make us happy in our own way without bothering about religion. God cannot give us happiness and peace apart from Himself, because it is not there. There is no such thing.

C.S. Lewis (1898-1963)

Your best shot at happiness, self-worth and personal satisfaction—the things that constitute real success—is not in earning as much as you can but in performing as well as you can something that you consider worthwhile. Whether that is healing the sick, giving hope to the hopeless, adding to the beauty of the world, or saving the world from nuclear holocaust, I cannot tell you.

William Raspberry, *Columnist*

I believe that the key to fulfillment is commitment to honor and commitment to a higher sense of purpose. Happiness is a transient, momentary experience of this fulfillment. Contentment we will have plenty of after we are dead.

Dr. Michael J. Murphy, *Forensic Psychologist, Teacher, Writer*

I believe the secret to contentment and happiness is probably to treat everyone you meet in such a way that you never have any fear about meeting them again.

Edwin W. Edwards, *Former Governor of Louisiana*

THE KEY TO CONTENTMENT AND HAPPINESS

That all who are happy, are equally happy, is not true. A peasant and a philosopher may be equally satisfied, but not equally happy. Happiness consists in the multiplicity of agreeable consciousness. A peasant has not capacity for having equal happiness with a philosopher.

Samuel Johnson (1709-1784)

Behind the door of every contented, happy man there ought to be someone standing with a little hammer and continually reminding him with a knock that there are unhappy people, that however happy he may be, life will sooner or later show him its claws, and trouble will come to him—illness, poverty, losses, and then no one will see or hear him, just as now he neither sees nor hears others.

Anton Chekhov (1860-1904)

Happiness is equilibrium. Shift your weight. Equilibrium is pragmatic. You have to get everything into proportion. You compensate, rebalance yourself so that you maintain your angle to your world. When the world shifts, you shift.

Tom Stoppard, *Author*

Always leave something to wish for, otherwise you will be miserable from your very happiness.

Baltasar Gracian, (1601-1658)

It is always wise to stop wishing for things long enough to enjoy the fragrance of those now flowering.

Anonymous

THE KEY TO CONTENTMENT AND HAPPINESS

Joy is the emotion which accompanies our fulfilling our natures as human beings. It is based on the experience of one's identity as a being of worth and dignity.

Rollo May, *Psychiatrist*

Look into your own essence.

Seek your highest possible mission in life. Identify the unique mission that engages and commits your energies and your talents, your imagination and your resources, your aspirations, dreams and fantasies wholly, without reservation, in its service. Then, surrender yourself, your time, your thoughts, your feelings—and your life itself—until your mission is actualized in objective reality or until you leave this plane.

Burt Dubin, *Speaker, Marketing Specialist*

He who seeks only for applause from without has all his happiness in another's keeping.

Anonymous

Discover your uniqueness and learn to exploit it in a way that serves others and you are guaranteed success, happiness and prosperity. This sums up everything I have learned and is the essence of my success!

Larry Winget, *Author, Motivational Speaker*

Happy is the man who has broken the chains that hurt the mind, and has given up worrying once and for all.

Ovid (43 B.C.-17 A.D.)

Let us be of good cheer, remembering that the misfortunes hardest to bear are those which never happen.

James Russell Lowell, (1819-1891)

→ THE KEY TO CONTENTMENT AND HAPPINESS ←

PHOTO BY JAMES WILCOX

→ THE KEY TO CONTENTMENT AND HAPPINESS ←

Happiness or contentment for some involves the meeting of a specific need in their lives. I saw a miserable, ill, four year old boy who was with his dad in my clinic. He was whimpering and wanted his mother's comfort. He was calling quietly for her by name. I asked his young father, who appeared loving and concerned, where mom was. He said she had left six or eight months ago and was living across the state. He hadn't heard from her in a long time. It was just him and his son making a life together. The kid was talking as if he had just seen his mother. He wanted to be held. Happiness for him was his mother's arms.

I have a friend in business who has made little profit in the last few years. He has built up his company over the past ten years, has been written about in regional magazines and is well respected in the community. He has invested his life in this business. His financial debt is great. To him, happiness would be a change of fortune and a few years of financial success.

In the town where I live, a very pleasant 38 year old lady is fighting the battle against breast cancer. It has already spread to other areas of her body. Her devoted husband agonizes but probably feels somewhat helpless. She has four young children who truly need her to get well. She does her best to appear positive and well in their presence. Many folks in the community pray for her recovery. To her and the family, there would be great happiness if she could somehow, some way be totally cured.

It has been said that a lifetime of constant happiness would be pure hell. That of course is pure speculation as no person has ever had such a life. We all experience unhappiness and discontent. Perhaps it is necessary. If there is indeed a divine purpose in all things that occur on Earth then what is the reason for suffering, pain, sadness and poverty? What is the purpose of evil? Is it that it makes us better able to appreciate good when it finally wins out? Could it be that when things

THE KEY TO CONTENTMENT AND HAPPINESS

are ultimately made right, we can savor and better enjoy comfort, happiness and the fullness of life? But the endings are not always happy. Illness is not always followed by the much appreciated health. Often what follows is death. But even that is better than chronic suffering. If the contrasting happiness and good never come then we might feel we have suffered a great injustice—cheated in the big picture in regards to what we deserve. Indeed what is it in this fragile life that we do deserve?

Those who are spiritual believe there is a purpose to pain and suffering. God has it all under control. He has a plan. At least He allows it to happen. But if the bad experiences are to teach us lessons or build our character then how long should we be made to suffer. We know that we don't choose the length of our trials and tribulations. If we did they would always be extremely brief and any learning or effect on us would therefore be superficial and soon forgotten. So sometimes we must just have faith that God knows best.

Some cynics say there is no God. There is no external force that is in control. Things just happen, like the change of the seasons, like day to night to day again. The pendulum is in motion and swings back and forth—happiness to sadness, contentment to unrest, peace to conflict—forever it swings. Man is the ultimate power. To have the good, we must obtain it, they claim. So they pursue happiness with both hands. They fervently seek pleasure and run from pain. Life is short—play hard. The strong shall possess what they desire and the weak will get the leftovers. Contentment will come through possessions. Whoever has the most toys in the end will be fulfilled. But finally the winter comes, darkness falls. Inevitably, there is illness, emptiness and depression and no amount of self effort can remove it. The crisis brings hopelessness. Life suddenly has no meaning or purpose. The quest for pleasure and possessions is found to be a dead-end street.

If pain has a purpose then perhaps it could be tolerated. If some good would result from a negative experience then it might be endured, maybe even rationalized or justified. A bitter pill can be swallowed if it improves our condition. But pain and suffering without purpose is senseless cruelty. To admit that it has an objective is to say that some external force must be orchestrating it for our good. This wise teacher cannot be mortal man, but something greater. It must be God.

Certain trials and tribulations come into all of our lives. It may be an illness, financial down turn, or troubled relationship. Happiness comes in just surviving them. Our character strengthens and maturity increases as we do. And through that, contentment may come.

J. Taylor Starkey

The key to happiness in life is to strive for excellence in all you do, accept responsibility for yourself and your family and always serve the One greater than ourselves.

George W. Bush, *Governor of Texas*

The key to happiness is to be able to go to sleep at night believing that you have done some good for somebody during your waking hours.

Charles Rangel, *Congressman, New York*

Compare what you want with what you have, and you'll be unhappy; compare what you deserve with what you have, and you'll be happy.

Evan Esar

A happy life must be to a great extent a quiet life, for it is only in an atmosphere of quiet that true joy can live.

Bertrand Russell (1872-1970)

THE KEY TO CONTENTMENT AND HAPPINESS

PHOTO BY TAYLOR STARKEY

THE KEY TO CONTENTMENT AND HAPPINESS

Happiness is a decision one makes. It derives from contentment or peace of mind. Happiness is not what happens to you but how you happen to life. Happiness doesn't come from outside events but happiness comes from the inside out.

Dennis Mannering, *Author, Motivational Speaker*

No man is happy unless he believes he is.

George Sand (1803-1876)

The majority of men devote the greater part of their lives to making their remaining years unhappy.

Jean de La Bruyere (1645-1696)

If it makes you happy to be unhappy, then be unhappy.

Anonymous

A sound mind in a sound body, is a short but full description of a happy state in this world. He that has these two, has little more to wish for; and he that wants either of them, will be little the better for anything else.

John Locke (1632-1704)

The key to contentment is to be still . . . and know that He is God.

Steve Farrar, *Author, Speaker*

The secret of contentment and happiness is to avoid comparison—thank God for what He has given YOU!

Dan Bolin, *Author, Camp Director*

THE KEY TO CONTENTMENT AND HAPPINESS

Some cause happiness wherever they go; others whenever they go.

Oscar Wilde (1856-1900)

Never believe that anyone who depends on happiness is happy.

He who would be truly happy must think his own lot best, and so live with men, as considering that God sees him, and so speak to God, as if men heard him.

Lucius Seneca (4 B.C.-65 A.D.)

A happiness that is sought for ourselves alone can never be found: for a happiness that is diminished by being shared is not big enough to make us happy.

There is a false and momentary happiness in self-satisfaction, but it always leads to sorrow because it narrows and deadens our spirit. True happiness is found in unselfish love, a love which increases in proportion as it is shared. There is no end to the sharing of love, and, therefore, the potential happiness of such love is without limit. Infinite sharing is the law of God's inner life.

Yet there can never be happiness in compulsion. It is not enough for love to be shared: it must be shared freely. That is to say it must be given, not merely taken. Unselfish love that is poured out upon a selfish object does not bring perfect happiness: not because love requires a return or a reward for loving, but because it rests in the happiness of the beloved. And if the one loved receives love selfishly, the lover is not satisfied. He sees that his love has failed to make the beloved happy.

Thomas Merton, (1915-1968), *from NO MAN IS AN ISLAND*

Contentment is a pearl of great price.

Anonymous

THE KEY TO CONTENTMENT AND HAPPINESS

God has given each of us ability or talent. It may be the ability to sew a straight seam, organize a research project, act in a play, create art, convince others to buy products, construct buildings, or teach. Helping us discover our talent should be one of the main goals of education. Next, we need to find a job or career that utilizes our particular talent. When we work at something we're naturally good at . . . contentment, fulfillment and happiness automatically follow. For me, expressing my observations about life as a writer makes me very happy, fulfilled and contented. Chocolate chip cookies and naps work well also.

Patricia Lorenz, *Inspirational Writer, Speaker*

The key to contentment is to eat well, drink a good glass of wine, accept your position in life, and enjoy your work whatever that may be, for as long as God lets you live.

Striving after wisdom, wealth and pleasure is like chasing after the wind. It is folly.

King Solomon (Tenth Century B.C.), Ecclesiastes

Talk happiness. The world is sad enough without your woe. No path is wholly rough.

Ella Wheeler Wilcox (1850-1919)

It is neither wealth nor splendor, but tranquility and occupation, which give happiness.

Thomas Jefferson (1743-1826)

If I didn't have a happy and enthusiastic marriage and three children I admire, I would probably spend my time mowing the grass and pulling weeds. Life is too short for that.

Frank Keating, *Governor of Oklahoma*

➢ THE KEY TO CONTENTMENT AND HAPPINESS ➣

PHOTO BY JAMES WILCOX

➔ THE KEY TO CONTENTMENT AND HAPPINESS ←

The secret of happiness has been defined by someone as the progressive accomplishing of worthwhile goals. Ancient theologians used the term *summum bonum,* which means "the greatest good." They believed that the greatest good was the "beatific vision"—seeing God—the attainment of that condition of spirit and soul which would allow them to come into the presence of God, to talk to Him, to see Him, and to be with Him. That was the ultimate good and the ultimate happiness.

Happiness is not a warm puppy or a fire on a cold night. It is not the beach at dawn or the other things that people say would make them happy. The deep, deep happiness that transcends all else comes from knowing God and, in turn, from being known by Him. Happiness is communing with Him, hearing His voice, and knowing that the work you accomplish in life, whatever it is, is in fulfillment of His desire for you.

When you know and do these things, then you will begin to know perfect happiness.

Pat Robertson, *Author, Chairman of the Board of the Christian Broadcasting Network*

Happiness is a wine of the rarest vintage, and seems insipid to a vulgar taste.

Logan Pearsall Smith (1865-1946)

To be happy one must have a good stomach and a bad heart.

Bernard Fontenelle (1657-1757)

Happiness is nothing if it is not known, and very little if it is not envied.

Samuel Johnson (1709-1784)

➔ THE KEY TO CONTENTMENT AND HAPPINESS ✦

The key to contentment, fulfillment, and happiness in life is to learn the purpose of life (who we are and why we are here), to learn the difference between truth and confusion that looks like truth, to be a loving and caring partner in a continually improving marriage, to be a parent and friend who takes time to effectively listen and influence (realizing that telling isn't teaching), to figure out better ways to do worthwhile things and do them, to work hard improving ourselves and the world we live in, to be obedient to eternal laws, to do what's right instead of what seems desirable at a particular moment—and then to help others discover the truths we have learned.

Glen C. Griffin, M.D., *Author, Pediatrician,*
Chief Editor of Post Graduate Medicine

Don't worry about things—food, drink, and clothes. For you already have life and a body—and they are far more important than what to eat and wear. Look at the birds! They don't worry about what to eat—they don't need to sow or reap or store up food—for your heavenly Father feeds them. And you are far more valuable to Him than they are. Will all your worries add a single moment to your life?[1]

And why worry about your clothes? Look at the field lilies! Even King Solomon in all his glory was not clothed as beautifully as they. And if God cared so wonderfully for flowers that are here today and gone tomorrow, won't He surely care for you?

Don't be anxious about tomorrow for each day has enough worries of its own.

Live each day to simply serve others.

Jesus Christ (4 B.C.-29 A.D.)

---
[1] From *The Living Bible,* Tyndale House Publishers, 1971

→ THE KEY TO CONTENTMENT AND HAPPINESS ←

Happiness is eating hot buttered rolls, fresh out of the oven, dipped in honey, baked by my smiling grandmother whose greatest joy in life is to cook for her grand kids (and then sit and rock on the front porch with her apron on).

Happiness is getting to wear blue jeans to work on Friday.

Happiness is driving an old pickup with the windows rolled down.

Happiness is standing outside and feeling the fresh, cold gusts of the first cold front after a long, hot, humid summer in South Texas . . . and then going to a football game.

Happiness is holding your first baby, who was born only minutes before, is all bundled up except for one of his tiny pink feet sticking out, who is all wrinkled and shriveled but still the cutest infant that you have ever seen, and you're trying not to cry in front of your in-laws.

Happiness is riding your bike up a very long, high hill—even if you have to stop and walk some—and finally making it to the top, and then enjoying the view—and then coasting, coasting, coasting as fast as you dare, until you reach the bottom.

Happiness is going hiking, or fishing, or just exploring in the wilderness all day, and getting very hungry while you start your fire, because a campfire takes a lot longer to get going than your stove at home, then cooking out, and maybe telling a few scary stories to your kids.

Happiness is getting together with the family, laughing a lot and eating a big meal, then watching old home movies of when you were a kid (when you didn't know what a mortgage was and thought having a real job meant taking out the trash three times a week).

Contentment comes in truly enjoying the moments. Savor the simple experiences. Make memories.

J. Taylor Starkey

THE KEY TO CONTENTMENT AND HAPPINESS

PHOTO BY MICHAEL SPOONEYBARGER

THE KEY TO CONTENTMENT AND HAPPINESS

The key to contentment and happiness?
Be good to your tools—RRR!

Tim Allen, *Author, Actor on "Home Improvement"*

In the twenty plus years I have been traveling across the country speaking to men and women, church and business groups, I find many people seeking happiness. Yet few ever truly find it, as happiness is based on our circumstances—which are seldom as we would desire. However those who seek contentment or fulfillment are those who are happy as their pleasure comes from an inner source. I find that for myself, and for those with whom I come in contact, there are two key elements to this inner peace and joy. First, those who feel a supernatural direction or call upon their lives to accomplish a certain task or mission, find fulfillment in completing that role. Also, those whose daily duties fit with their inborn personality style find them easy and satisfying to accomplish, while those who are functioning in their weaknesses rather than their strengths are continually frustrated and exhausted.

Florence Littauer, *Speaker, Author*

Two men look out through the same bars;
One sees the mud, and one the stars . . . .

Frederick Langbridge (1849-1923)

My response regarding the key to contentment is very simple. The Holy Bible and my faith in God are two principles I have held closely for a lifetime. I cannot imagine life without either.

Kirk Fordice, *Governor of Mississippi*

→ THE KEY TO CONTENTMENT AND HAPPINESS ←

The secret of life lies in the cultivation of character. It is the little things that we do daily that add up to a fortune in the end. Patience, persistence, human kindness and empathy practiced on a daily basis eventually lead to the formation of healthy habits. Healthy habits are the cornerstones of character, and it is character that finally determines the destiny of each of us.

Destiny is done
One day at a time.
Polish and perfect
The timeless qualities
That are the Distinguishing Marks
Of the extraordinary Human Being

D. Trinidad Hunt, *Speaker, Author, Corporate Trainer*

When I have something that causes me concern, I just dismiss everything connected with it from my mind and let my work absorb me. It's surprising how it clears up.

Henry Ward Beecher (1813-1887)

The key to happiness is doing something you love to do, someone to love, and something to look forward to. With these ingredients a happy life is ensured.

Mary Kay Ash, *Chairman Emeritus, Mary Kay Cosmetics*

I don't know that there is one key, but I find happiness through my faith, my family, my friends, my values, and by doing the best I can do in Congress on the issues I care about.

Henry A. Waxman, *U.S. Congressman, California*

The key to contentment is to define a philosophy and goals and make some effort and progress towards reaching those goals.

Craig Thomas, *U.S. Congressman, Wyoming*

THE KEY TO CONTENTMENT AND HAPPINESS

I have now reigned about fifty years in victory or peace, beloved by my subjects, dreaded by my enemies, and respected by my allies. Riches and honors, power and pleasure, have waited on my call, nor does any earthly blessing appear to have been wanting to my felicity. In this situation, I have diligently numbered the days of pure and genuine happiness which have fallen to my lot; they amount to fourteen. O man, place not thy confidence in this present world!

Abd-er-Rahman III, *Former King of Spain*

The happiness of a married man depends on the people he has not married.

Oscar Wilde (1856-1900)

Happiness: a good bank account, a good cook, and a good digestion.

Jean Jacques Rousseau (1712-1778)

If you want to be happy for an hour—
watch a great movie.
If you want to be happy for a day—
buy or sell a boat.
If you want to be happy for a month—
get married or divorced.
If you want to be happy for a year—
win the lottery.
If you want to be happy for a lifetime—
find a way to make a difference.

Mike Buettell, *Speaker, School Counselor*

There is no way to happiness. Happiness is the way.

Wayne Dyer

➢ THE KEY TO CONTENTMENT AND HAPPINESS ➢

PHOTO BY BRAD ALLERTON

→ THE KEY TO CONTENTMENT AND HAPPINESS ←

I believe the key to contentment, fulfillment or happiness in life is learning the balance between "high intention and low attachment." It is the integration between the western philosophy of pursuing your heartfelt dreams with passion and persistence, and the eastern philosophy of accepting life, yourself, and other people the way they are. It is the integration of the masculine and feminine aspects of one's self: making things bigger and letting things be.

When one achieves this integration, full contentment is possible. I learn to listen to my inner voice (the voice of God), follow my heart, do the best I can, accept what happens and rejoice in the abundance that my life offers. I become one with all aspects of me, all aspects of others, and all aspects of the universe. I accept the moving, changing cycles of nature, myself, and everything else. It becomes a dance, a dynamic interplay between all the different dimensions of my beingness. How does one accomplish this? Again, by developing both one's will and one's ability to surrender, one's ability to be self-disciplined and one's ability to flow. When one develops true self-awareness, you automatically know which one to do in which situation. You become one with yourself, with others, with your environment and with life and God.

Jack Canfield, *Motivational Speaker, Consultant,*
Co-Author of CHICKEN SOUP FOR THE SOUL

If very early in life one can accept the premise that the only guarantee we have is "There will be change," then perhaps one can live in harmony knowing that All is temporary. One must also learn to listen to the small voice inside and follow only where one's soul leads. And when someone starts to say, "What you need to do is . . ." then run like hell in the opposite direction!

Sharon Steen

THE KEY TO CONTENTMENT AND HAPPINESS

Nothing flatters a man as much as the happiness of his wife; he is always proud of himself as the source of it.
Samuel Johnson (1709-1784)

A man who finds no satisfaction in himself, seeks for it in vain elsewhere.
Duc Francois de La Rochefoucauld, (1613-1680)

Inner joy is a power source. The better you feel, the more you can draw on your natural energy and ability. There is a crucial difference between the pleasure of getting something you want and the inner joy that empowers you to go after it in the first place. The first is an effect, the second is the cause. Inner joy is different from passing experiences of pleasure or excitement. It is your internal state before you act, your baseline experience of living, the emotional ground on which you stand, day in and day out.
Harold H. Bloomfield M.D., *Author, Speaker, Psychological Educator*

Happy are those who live in the dream of their own existence, and see all things in the light of their own minds; who walk by faith and hope; to whom the guiding star of their youth still shines from afar, and into whom the spirit of the world has not entered!
William Hazlitt (1778-1830)

The belief that youth is the happiest time of life is founded on a fallacy. The happiest person is the person who thinks the most interesting thoughts, and we grow happier as we grow older.
William Lyon Phelps (1865-1943)

THE KEY TO CONTENTMENT AND HAPPINESS

Helping others is the key to contentment, fulfillment and happiness in life. The desire to help other people is one of the glues that holds society together. By making this a long term philosophy, my life is continually enriched by my interactions with others.

Thomas R. Carper, *Governor of Delaware*

Content lodges oftener in cottages than palaces.

Thomas Fuller (1608-1661)

Discovering God's will in terms of your giftedness and His call upon your life is the key to contentment. As it says in Phillipians in the Bible, don't worry or be anxious about anything, but pray about everything and tell God what you need, and be thankful for His answers. Then you will experience God's peace which surpasses all human understanding.

Howard G. Hendricks, *Speaker, Seminary Professor*

The longevity of life is so uncertain that I firmly believe an individual must live his life to its fullest. A person should and must begin each day of their life with a very positive attitude. Beginning each day in a happy and excited mode is not only invigorating to you as the person, but enables you to make others feel good and excited about the things they do in their realm of life. I have found that it takes so much more to create a negative image than a positive one so I try to face each day in the proper mode. My hope is what I do on this good earth will also account for where I have the opportunity to spend my eternity, while at the same time making others feel good as well.

Gaylan Duncan, *Funeral Director*

❥ THE KEY TO CONTENTMENT AND HAPPINESS ❦

PHOTO BY FRANK TILLEY

THE KEY TO CONTENTMENT AND HAPPINESS

You've got ten thousand things to do, and you are desperately trying to get one of them done when the baby starts crying and you realize that you have to drop everything and rock that baby. And as you rock that baby you might sing a little Mother Goose. Pretty soon the baby starts to relax, then you start to relax. The baby is making little cooing sounds—you're humming some Goose—and WHAM, right out of the blue you realize, man it doesn't get any better than this. You have connected with the cosmos and my God you are contented. For me happiness is like that. It comes in small packages when I least expect it and usually when I am up to my hip pockets in alligators.

Joe Scruggs, *Songwriter, Children's Entertainer*

Ignorance is the key to everything in life.
An ignorant person in constantly surprised.

Forrest Gump **by Winston Groom**

One must be perfectly stupid to be perfectly happy.

Anonymous

Knowing that I have family and friends who genuinely care for me has filled my life with happiness and contentment and helped me "over the hills and through the valleys." Involvement with diverse groups and interesting activities has been the "key" to my fulfillment.

Sandra S. Williams, *Mother, Civic Leader*

I'm not sure about the key to happiness, but I suspect you won't find it if you worry about it too much.

Robert Bartley, *Editor, The Wall Street Journal*

Happiness for me is largely a matter of digestion.

Lin Yutang (1895-1976)

THE KEY TO CONTENTMENT AND HAPPINESS

...erm happiness or fulfillment does not come from gaining material possessions, achieving the perfect job, or obtaining great wealth. This is a false hope that many people have. It is the underlying theme in much of the advertising that constantly bombards us. The thought is that if one purchased this item or performed this certain action that demonstrated their desired social status, then and only then would they be happy. But once that action is done or thing is obtained, the joy is found to be only transient, and so the search continues.

The advertisers promise us all sorts of things, either directly or in a subliminal way. Drink this beer and life will be a party. Drive this car and you will look good and be happy. Wear these clothes and you will achieve the lifestyle and make the statement that you desire. Shop at our store and find everything you need at the price you want and you will be at least content if you don't reach total nirvana. Whoever said that money can't buy happiness never shopped at our store!

If gaining wealth and possessions caused contentment then those who have it all would be much happier than the rest of us. We know that is not true. The rich are usually no more, and often perhaps less fulfilled than those of humble means, particularly if their happiness is dependent on their possessions.

A shiny new car brings happiness for a year or so, until the next year's model comes out with approximately 328 new safety and engineering improvements. A huge new house can be exciting until one becomes burdened with the cost of the mortgage, taxes, and maintenance. Even that fantastic view out the front window or off the back deck loses its constant appeal after awhile and becomes something that only awes or impresses the infrequent visitors.

Happiness or contentment is not the destination, it is the journey. It is not the hidden treasure at the end but rather the expedition. It is not the dead animal but rather the hunt. It is not the end— only the means.

J. Taylor Starkey

THE KEY TO CONTENTMENT AND HAPPINESS

Two spiritual truths stand out in my experience as practical guides for life. First, that we are all connected, with the practical result that only through loving others may I demonstrate my self-love. Second, that my external experience is a true reflection of my internal condition, meaning that only through peace on the inside can I experience joy and fulfillment on the outside. When I practice these truths, I find things may not always go my way, but they always go to my benefit.

Marion Barry, Jr. , *Mayor of Washington, D.C.*

It has always struck me as remarkable that in a survey reported in "Psychology Today" many years ago, wealth did not seem to affect the level of people's happiness. Around the world, whether impoverished or affluent, the general level of happiness was the same. The researchers found just one major difference: whether one had more or less than one's neighbor.

The Bible says godliness with contentment is great gain. Having a sense of gratitude, which can surely be found in a relationship with Christ, generates happiness despite circumstances.

Harold Myra, *Author, President of Christianity Today Magazine*

Time is the inexplicable raw material of everything. With it, all is possible; without it, nothing. The supply of time is truly a daily miracle, an affair genuinely astonishing when one examines it. You wake up each morning, and lo! your purse is magically filled with twenty-four hours of the unmanufactured tissue of the universe of your life! You have to live on this twenty-four hours of daily time. Out of it you have to spin health, pleasure, money, contentment, respect, and the evolution of your immortal soul. Its right use, its most effective use, is a matter of the highest urgency and of the most thrilling actuality. All depends on that. Your happiness depends on that.

Arnold Bennett (1867-1931)

→ THE KEY TO CONTENTMENT AND HAPPINESS ←

PHOTO BY MICHAEL SPOONEYBARGER

THE KEY TO CONTENTMENT AND HAPPINESS

The key to contentment is to be living an on-purpose life with passion, manifesting the genius which was coded within our DNA/RNA at birth.
**Mark Victor Hansen, *Speaker*,
Co-Author of Chicken Soup for the Soul**

Look at a day when you are supremely satisfied at the end. It's not a day when you lounge around doing nothing; it's when you've had everything to do, and you've done it.
Margaret Thatcher, *former Prime Minister of Great Britain*

When I was young I thought money was the most important thing in life; now that I am old I know that it is.
Oscar Wilde (1856-1900)

It occurs to me that the key to contentment, happiness, and fulfillment is simple—just be truthful to God, yourself, and others. It could be more complicated than that if someone wanted to make it so.
David Barnhart, *Banker*

Happy are all who perfectly follow the laws of God. Happy are all who search for God, and always do His will, rejecting compromise with evil, and walking only in His paths.
Psalm 119, The Living Bible

The secret of happiness is not in doing what one likes, but in liking what one has to do.
Sir James M. Barrie (1860-1937)

We exaggerate misfortune and happiness alike. We are never either so wretched or so happy as we say we are.
Honore de Balzac (1799-1850)

THE KEY TO CONTENTMENT AND HAPPINESS

The key to contentment?
Faith, hope, love, and perseverance!

Oliver North, *Author, Speaker*

The key to contentment, fulfillment, or happiness in life is probably not the same thing for any two people—otherwise, folks probably wouldn't spend so much time looking for it, and have such a hard time finding it. I don't pretend to have any answers. But I suspect the key may lie outside ourselves. The times I've been most content, most fulfilled, and happiest were the times I felt most certain I'd done something for someone else: for my mother and father, brother and sister, wife and children, for my community, my country, my God.

Dan Rather, *CBS News Anchor & Managing Editor*

I am more and more convinced that our happiness or unhappiness depends far more on the way we meet the events of life than on the nature of those events themselves.

Wilhelm Von Humboldt, (1767-1835)

I believe the key to contentment, fulfillment and happiness comes from surrounding yourself with family and friends throughout your life to create, share, and relive memories. The most important moments in my life have been those which were shared with loved ones. They made the experiences even more special.

J. Robert Kerrey, *U.S. Senator, Nebraska*

For every ailment under the sun
There is a remedy, or there is none;
If there be one, try to find it;
If there be none, never mind it.

Mother Goose Rhyme

THE KEY TO CONTENTMENT AND HAPPINESS

"What is the key to contentment, fulfillment, or happiness in life?"

What a task to answer that in a paragraph! Happiness comes not from a single thing but many things; I like to think of multiple tracks, some short-term, some long-term, all operating at the same time. A sine qua non of happiness, I believe, is a reciprocal bond with another, a bond that gets demonstrated regularly if not frequently.

That's necessary—but not sufficient. Also most helpful: A philosophy that acknowledges seasons, ebb and flow, a cycle of life and energy.

The knowledge of personal resilience, which implies having had some knocks (but not crushing blows) along the way and having developed the wherewithal to survive setbacks. The proven ability to make one's living by one's own wits or efforts, not be just a cog in someone else's wheel. The experience of having done something bold—knowing that you can make a difference. I personally believe that raising children is essential for a dimension of happiness not even knowable any other way—though they are certainly the ultimate long-term track; they give life depth, humility, and a positive tie to the future. Also knowing that one's children get along with each other is an extraordinarily deep source of contentment as well; I think because it is an assurance that they will go through life with at least one close relationship, and because it affirms that the family was there, that it had an effect. On a whole other track are what might be called little pleasures—a good massage, an exhilarating walk in the country, a letter from a friend. And lastly, something vastly underestimated by the middle and upper classes—money; it certainly can't buy happiness, but freedom from constant worry about where the rent money will come from or how the children will be fed is probably essential.

Hara Estroff Marano, *Editor, Psychology Today*

➤ THE KEY TO CONTENTMENT AND HAPPINESS ❖

PHOTO BY TAYLOR STARKEY

THE KEY TO CONTENTMENT AND HAPPINESS

The secret of happiness and contentment is doing something for a living that you would do for free, something that constantly challenges you personally and professionally; being in a position where you can enjoy but never totally relax; always having something to look forward to; scintillating, stimulating conversation with good friends.

Patricia Fripp, *Motivational Speaker*

It has been well said that no man ever sank under the burden of the day. It is when tomorrow's burden is added to the burden of today that the weight is more than a man can bear.

George MacDonald (1824-1905)

The basis for contentment and fulfillment seems to change as we mature and grow older. For the young, it is most apt to be based on short term experiences, but as we age it is more dependent upon the degree to which we feel we have fulfilled our dreams and ambitions, and whether or not we feel we have made a difference in the world by having been here.

Robert W. Reasoner, *Author, Educator, Speaker*

What is the key to happiness and contentment? Beer.

Dave Barry, *Author, Columnist*

The secret of being miserable is to have the leisure to bother about whether you are happy or not.

George Bernard Shaw (1856-1950)

Happiness is having all of your objections sustained.

Timothy Fults, *Attorney*

Variety is the spice of life.

William Cowper (1731-1800)

THE KEY TO CONTENTMENT AND HAPPINESS

Unless each day can be looked back upon by an individual as one in which he had some fun, some joy, some real satisfaction, that day is a loss. It is unchristian and wicked, in my opinion, to allow such a thing to occur.

Dwight D. Eisenhower (1890-1969)

When I was 30 years old and very unhappy my father said something to me that I will never forget. He said the "Declaration of Independence" grants us the inalienable right to the pursuit of happiness. It does not give us the right to be happy. Those words have been my cornerstone for happiness ever since.

Maury Povich, *TV Talk Show Host*

My life has taught me that fulfillment, contentment, and happiness are never found in things, but in service to others. Acts of kindness, the Talmud tells us, are the source of the meaningfulness in our lives. Make the world a little bit better for someone other than yourself and you'll sleep better. Ease the burden for another being and your burden will seem lighter too.

Hanoch McCarty, Ed.D, *Educator, Author, Motivational Speaker*

Keep your face to the sunshine and you cannot see the shadow.

Helen Keller (1880-1968)

The secret of happiness is this: Let your interests be as wide as possible, and let your reactions to the things and persons that interest you be as far as possible friendly rather than hostile.

Bertrand Russell (1872-1970)

→ THE KEY TO CONTENTMENT AND HAPPINESS ←

A secret to happiness is diversion or change. Life is dynamic. Getting into a monotonous rut can create great discontent. That is not to say that a degree of stability is not desirable in many areas. One's marriage, home life, vocation, and relationships with friends and family members should show constancy and commitment. But even then, healthy change must occur.

Nothing, if examined closely, stays the same. We don't and the people and things around us don't. We may sometimes close our eyes and ears and not see changes occurring. To remain in perfect balance and harmonious tune, adjustments must be made. If your relationships with your spouse or your kids have not deepened or matured in the last several years then they may have lost much of the joy. If your job has involved no change, no new responsibility and no new learning for as long as you can remember then you may well be unhappy. On the other hand, work and personal relationships can gain new vitality if we put forth the effort to make positive, necessary changes in them.

Variety may well be the spice of life but dedication and commitment is the meat and potatoes. Long term happiness usually doesn't come through an exciting new job, a new marriage to someone seemingly more understanding, or new friends who are perhaps more interesting, but often rather through intentional growth in those areas as they currently exist. Change for the better can create happiness.

I once had the occasion to sit along a busy Texas highway on a Friday evening while waiting for a ride. I was amused to see all of the people traveling south with their boats in tow, leaving the rocky elevations of the Hill Country and heading for the coast. They were full of smiles and anticipation. At the same time traveling north from the coast were anxious and excited families in station wagons and suburbans pulling campers towards their Hill Country destinations.

It is interesting to note that people who have lived in idyl-

❖ THE KEY TO CONTENTMENT AND HAPPINESS ❖

PHOTO BY MYRA STARKEY

lic settings for a period of time soon quit being awed by the beauty that surrounds them. Even those who reside in resort areas often get dulled to the scenery and entertainment and certainly don't have the same appreciation as the tourists.

Sometimes a brief change in environment is all that it takes to brighten your outlook. If you live on the coast, go to the mountains. If you are tired of the heat, travel to a cooler climate. If you are fatigued by the hectic, crowded city, then go to the country. But wherever you go, just don't forget your way back home.

J. Taylor Starkey

The key to contentment or fulfillment in life is in knowing and relating to God who created us and gave himself so that we could reach the potential for which we were created.

John Ashcroft, *Senator, Missouri*

My view is the simple traditional one: happiness cannot be attained by direct pursuit. Indeed, attempts to pursue it generally lead to the pursuer being unhappy, dissatisfied and wondering "Is that all there is?"

Happiness seems to arrive most reliably as a by-product of pursuing other things—generally the welfare of others, work, or the will of God as we can best judge it. Often the happy man is so busy or preoccupied with the fortunes of others that he does not consciously realize that he is happy.

John O'Sullivan, *Editor, National Review Magazine*

Happiness is the goal of every normal human being. As it is given to few men to die happy, the best that man can hope and strive and pray for is momentary happiness during life, repeated as frequently as the cards allow.

George Jean Nathan (1882-1958)

THE KEY TO CONTENTMENT AND HAPPINESS

The chief thing you are seeking in this world is happiness; and happiness does not depend upon good health or money or fame, though good health is a large factor. It depends, however, principally on one thing only: your thoughts. If you can't have what you want, be grateful for what you have. Keep thinking constantly of all the big things you have to be thankful for instead of complaining about the little things that annoy you.

Dale Carnegie (1888-1955)

We take greater pains to persuade others that we are happy, than in endeavoring to be so ourselves.

Oliver Goldsmith (1728-1774)

PEACE isn't the absence of conflict or disease— it is the ability to deal with it.

SECURITY is an illusion. The only real security comes from God.

CONTROL is a superstition. You only have control over yourself. And remember, when you feel trapped or beaten down, you still have control over your choices.

Peace of mind is the goal.

Naomi Judd, *Singer, Songwriter*

The key to contentment is turning your life over to God, have faith, and trust that He is in control.

Tom Landry, *Former Coach, Dallas Cowboys*

Happiness lies in the consciousness we have of it, and by no means in the way the future keeps its promises.

George Sand (1803-1876)

➔ THE KEY TO CONTENTMENT AND HAPPINESS ←

Our happiness often depends on how we look at things. C.S. Lewis commented that life is viewed by some as a hotel and by others as a prison. Those who see it as a hotel may often be quite unhappy and disillusioned, while those who view it as a jail may think that it generally isn't too bad of a place. People who expect a life filled with room service, bellhops, a daily maid to clean up your messes, and a room with a great view may find that real life is a disappointment. Conversely, individuals may be more content with the way things are if they realize that life, like a prison, can sometimes be confining, monotonous and mundane, that you have to clean up after yourself, that the food is not always so great and the people not always so nice and honest. Those realists who can avoid pessimism often find that even though they may be "doing time" and "paying their debt to society," life is filled with unexpected joys, frequent beauty, sunny days, undeserved kindness from friends and strangers, steadfast love, rainbows, golden sunsets, and occasional mountaintop experiences.

J. Taylor Starkey

Human felicity or happiness is produced not so much by great pieces of good fortune that seldom happen, but by little advantages that occur every day.

Benjamin Franklin (1706-1790), *from* AUTOBIOGRAPHY

The mind is its own place, and in itself can make a heaven of Hell, a hell of Heaven.

John Milton (1608-1674)

Few things are necessary to make the wise man happy, but nothing satisfies the fool—and this is the reason why so many of mankind are miserable.

Duc Francois de La Rochefoucauld (1613-1680)

❧ THE KEY TO CONTENTMENT AND HAPPINESS ❦

PHOTO BY FRANK TILLEY

THE KEY TO CONTENTMENT AND HAPPINESS

Put a big, broad, honest-to-God smile on your face; throw back your shoulders; take a good deep breath, and sing a snatch of a song. If you can't sing, whistle. If you can't whistle, hum. You will quickly discover that it is physically impossible to remain blue or depressed while you are acting out the symptoms of being radiantly happy!

Dale Carnegie (1888-1955)

All real and wholesome enjoyments possible to man have been just as possible to him since first he was made of the earth as they are now; and they are possible to him chiefly in peace. To watch the corn grow, and the blossoms set; to draw hard breath over plowshare or spade; to read, to think, to love, to hope, to pray—these are the things that make men happy.... Now and then a wearied king, or a tormented slave, found out where the true kingdoms of the world were, and possessed himself, in a furrow or two of garden ground, a truly infinite dominion.

John Ruskin (1819-1900)

For me, the key to contentment, fulfillment, or happiness in life is my acceptance (only this summer), in my heart or the core of my being, that God loves Me, as I am, warts and all. And with that acceptance, at age sixty, I am really at peace with my life and vocation. This required moving from my head to my heart. I knew, but did not accept it.

Russ Matthews, *Episcopal Minister*

Happiness is the overcoming of not unknown obstacles toward a known goal and, transiently, the contemplation of or indulgence in pleasure.

L. Ron Hubbard, *from* D*IANETICS*

THE KEY TO CONTENTMENT AND HAPPINESS

The creed which accepts as the foundations of morals "utility" or the "greatest happiness principle" holds that actions are right in proportion as they tend to promote happiness, wrong as the tend to produce the reverse of happiness. By happiness is intended pleasure, and the absence of pain; by unhappiness, pain, and the privation of pleasure. Pleasure and freedom from pain are the only things desirable as ends. It is quite compatible with the principle of utility to recognize the fact that some kinds of pleasure are more desirable and more valuable than others.

Few human creatures would consent to be changed into any of the lower animals for a promise of the fullest allowance of a beast's pleasures; no intelligent human being would consent to be a fool, no instructed person an ignoramus, no person of feeling and conscience would be selfish and base, even though they should be persuaded that the fool, the dunce, or the rascal is better satisfied with his lot than they are with theirs. A being of higher faculties requires more to make him happy, is capable probably of more acute suffering, and certainly accessible to it at more points, than one of an inferior type; but in spite of these liabilities, he can never really wish to sink into what he feels to be a lower grade of existence. It is undisputable that the being whose capacities of enjoyment are low has the greatest chance of having them fully satisfied; and a highly endowed being will always feel that any happiness which he can look for, as the world is constituted, is imperfect. It is better to be a human being dissatisfied than a pig satisfied; better to be Socrates dissatisfied than a fool satisfied. And if the fool, or the pig, are of a different opinion, it is because they only know their own side of the question. The other party to the comparison knows both sides.

John Stuart Mill (1806-1873), *from Utilitarianism*

→ THE KEY TO CONTENTMENT AND HAPPINESS ←

It is unlikely that one would be contented or fulfilled if they did not feel that they were living up to their potential. For instance, a school teacher may have a desire to be a writer. A salesman might feel like he should own his own business. A junior vice president in a corporation might think he or she should be the president. A doctor might want to be a lawyer or vice versa. A mother may feel compelled to leave the home to pursue a career. Whatever that person had been doing for years, and perhaps was happy in that task, may all of the sudden find it routine, mundane and boring.

Obviously this career discontent can cause problems as the person and his or her family may already be settled into their home, community, and lifestyle and the willingness to make a drastic change may be lacking. So the person decides to just do the best they can and tolerate their job. And slowly their lack of contentment may worsen as they quit fully investing themselves in their work.

It should be expected that any function of work would eventually lose some of its initial excitement. Anything done over and over again would become less of a thrill. I suspect that even heart surgeons or race car drivers don't leap out of bed with keen anticipation every morning. Occupations such as those have their tense moments of crisis, just like many jobs do, but are probably generally filled with repetition and routine. As a parent, holding your new baby has got to be one of the greatest mountain top experiences in life, but the actual year after year raising and disciplining of children has its share of marching through dark valleys. No activity in life is perpetually fascinating, stimulating, and enjoyable.

A lack of fulfillment in one's job is a very typical feeling in a person in their thirties or older who is suffering a mid-life crisis. In fact, it would be helpful if they spend a minute or two mentioning that at commencement exercises. The speaker might say, "Congratulations on your graduation, enjoy your career . . . and by the way, if you wake up one morning about

➢ THE KEY TO CONTENTMENT AND HAPPINESS ➢

PHOTO BY BRAD ALLERTON

THE KEY TO CONTENTMENT AND HAPPINESS

10 to 15 years from now and don't want to go to work anymore . . . well, just remember you are not the first person to feel that way. It's just a mid-life crisis. Hang in there! Try not to do anything crazy. You'll get over it."

When you are personally experiencing this career crisis and are truly unhappy, it is hard to know what to do. Even if you do realize that it might be just a stage you are going through, it is difficult to feel content. And what if you really should be doing something else to which you would be better suited?

Many of us sometimes fail to appreciate the importance of our job. We may not realize the positive impact we have on people around us, either our customers, clients, or co-workers. If we have anyone who works under us then we probably directly determine their satisfaction in life. Chances are, if our job was not essential, we wouldn't be paid for doing it and it would be phased out. For those whose job is teaching or raising children, there is no higher calling as our society's future rests on their shoulders.

When you begin to notice yourself becoming weary of your daily tasks, there should be two areas that you focus on. First, think of ways that you can improve, update, or modernize your methods or techniques. Examine your specific function and look for ways to be more creative. Second, work on your relationships with your co-workers and customers. Determine that you will sincerely care about, serve, and take an unselfish interest in them. That can be really refreshing.

It is okay to pursue dreams. If your career dissatisfaction is not just part of a mid-life crisis, then that desire for change won't go away. You may end up trying something new. But don't do anything rash. Talk to a lot of people. Ask a lot of questions. Check into job availability. Read some books. Take some classes. Test the waters before you jump in over your head. You never know, the grass may be greener on your side of the fence.

J. Taylor Starkey

→ THE KEY TO CONTENTMENT AND HAPPINESS ←

By working on knowledge, skill, and desire, the intersection of which could be defined as habit, we can break through to new levels of personal and interpersonal effectiveness as we break with old paradigms that may have been a source of pseudo-security for years.

It's sometimes a painful process. It's a change that has to be motivated by a higher purpose, by the willingness to subordinate what you think you want now for what you want later. But this process produces happiness, "the object and design of our existence." Happiness can be defined, in part at least, as the fruit of the desire and ability to sacrifice what we want now for what we want eventually.

Stephen Covey, *from THE SEVEN HABITS OF HIGHLY EFFECTIVE PEOPLE*

I believe the key to contentment, fulfillment, and happiness in life is the ability to set goals, follow your principles, and to keep your word.

George Allen, *Governor of Virginia*

A group of boys and girls were asked to list the things that made them happiest. Their answers were rather touching. Here is the boys' list: "A swallow flying; looking into deep, clear water; water being cut at the bow of a boat; a fast train rushing; a builder's crane lifting something heavy; my dog's eyes."

And here is what the girls said made them happy: "street lights on the river; red roofs in the trees; smoke rising from a chimney; red velvet; the moon in the clouds." There is something in the beautiful essence of the universe that is expressed, though only half-articulated, by these things. To become a happy person have a clean soul, eyes that see romance in the commonplace, a child's heart and spiritual simplicity.

Norman Vincent Peale,
from THE POWER OF POSITIVE THINKING (1952)

→ THE KEY TO CONTENTMENT AND HAPPINESS ←

Your request regarding the key to contentment is an unusual one. I am reminded of a dozen old jokes about guys seeking the secret of life from aged gurus on Himalayan mountaintops.

Contentment, fulfillment, and happiness in life all came to me at different times. I was a miserable teenager and could not wait to become an adult. I ruined my face in a racing accident at age twenty-four and further retarded the process. My first marriage festered for twenty years before coming completely apart. But I was moving steadily toward those three goals throughout that often painful process.

I believe that all of us must do the work that we are good at, that gives us pleasure, but—more fundamentally—I'm convinced that laughter is the key to contentment, fulfillment and happiness in my life. I suppose miserable people can laugh but not very convincingly. In my marriage, in my friendships, and in my work, I seek fun. If some part of my life isn't fun, I'm inclined to the belief that there's something wrong with it. If that thing can't be fixed, then I should walk away from it. During the past twenty years, adherence to this principle has forced me to leave a job I loved, a job I regarded as the best I would ever have, but that was the only bad thing that's happened to me. I recovered, started a new magazine, and laughed a lot in the process. Each time I read the obituary of some famous person or powerful person, I wonder if they had as much fun as I 'm having. When I finally shoot through, my only regret will be for further good times that I may be about to miss.

You should also be aware of Nelson Algren's advice to young writers which went: Never play cards with a man called Doc. Never eat in a place called Mom's. Never sleep with a woman whose troubles are worse than your own.

David E. Davis, Jr., *Editor/Publications Director,*
Automobile Magazine

➔ THE KEY TO CONTENTMENT AND HAPPINESS ❖

PHOTO BY FRANK TILLEY

THE KEY TO CONTENTMENT AND HAPPINESS

To be happy is not the purpose of our being, but to deserve happiness.
Immanuel Hermann von Fichte

Happiness makes up in height for what it lacks in length.
Robert Frost (1874-1963)

Your question has been posed to the right person as I am a very happy woman after 39 years of marriage. I am very fulfilled as my home is a traffic jam of family, grandchildren, and friends. These include friends from the business community and friends from the Christian community of which I am a part.

I am contented with the way my life is, (by my own decision), a place where guilt is not harbored. My personal philosophy: Lead a guilt free life. In taking this stand, all ethical and moral decisions come easily and have led to contentment.

Peace of mind precedes happiness and happiness comes from knowing God is in control and allowing God to take control of my life as well as my talent.

Am I rich? . . . that's for my banker to decide. Am I successful? Yes, beyond a shadow of a doubt because contentment, fulfillment and happiness spell success.
Bobbie Gee, *Speaker/Consultant*

The key to contentment is good health and a clear conscience.
Brereton C. Jones, *Governor of Kentucky*

Health is the greatest of all possessions; a pale cobbler is better than a sick king.
Isaac Bickerstaffe (1735-1812)

→ THE KEY TO CONTENTMENT AND HAPPINESS ←

True joy is where you live. It's on your side of the fence. Happiness thrives in your neighborhood or town and it can be a great place to live.

Sure, there is hate, envy and strife in your city. People closing their ears and their minds to others seeking their attention. But there are romantic souls who fall in love each day. New love is not just for fuzzy-headed young fools. Others, having mindlessly plunged into love long ago, now renew their devotion with delightful new discoveries or revelations about their mate. Some just sit in warm, relaxed contentment in each other's presence.

Still, there is the sadness and tragedy of murder, assault, and rape in your town—the paper says it happens. The obituaries list many deaths from accidents, illness, or old age. Friends and families weep. It was just too sudden—didn't expect it would happen so soon. Elsewhere now there are new arrivals—eight pounds, six ounces—mom and baby doing well—father beaming—didn't have the chance to read the paper or notice the weather. And in section three, new couples were married—left yesterday for the honeymoon at the beach—holding hands often and longing for each other, still not believing they get to spend their lives together.

Even now, old friends in your town disappoint each other—one too many times—and their friendship falls apart. Over time they may even grow bitter towards each other. It just didn't turn out like they thought it would. It seems you just can't trust people. They'll always let you down in the end. Yet other friends laugh and joke. They cherish the memories of fun times of years past, adventures had, happy times, sad seasons—repeating old stories. They can't really remember having an argument or disagreement that amounted to much in all these years. They look forward to experiences to come. There's nothing like old friends. In your neighborhood, some people build higher walls and fences, others chat over low fences, and others tear down fences thinking it looks nice for

→ THE KEY TO CONTENTMENT AND HAPPINESS ←

it to be like one big yard all together.

Yes, there are kids joining gangs in your city. Young teens have just been told they are pregnant. Many juveniles are into drugs and alcohol—they like the feeling and only in intoxication do they escape the emotional pain, loneliness, insecurity and uncertainty in their lives. But next door a contented child sits in her mother's willing lap, being read her favorite book for the umpteenth time. A father and his sons whoop it up in the ballpark. A scout troop eagerly packs up for their camp out. Angelic, harmonious voices rise from a youth choral group. The home-team offensive line blocks the rush, the quarterback connects with the tight-end racing down the sideline, the crowd jumps to its feet and cheers wildly.

It all happens in your town; the good, the bad, the pure, the evil, the love, the hate, the well-intentioned and that of ill will. Ambulances and police cars blast down some roads with sirens blaring while on other streets ice cream trucks move lazily along playing their jingles. Big cities to small towns—it's all there. Make a difference where you can to change all for the better. The place where you live is what you make of it.

J. Taylor Starkey

The key to living in "Paradise" in your lifetime is to know how magnificent this universe is, and that as an integral part of the universe, all beings, regardless of their behaviors, actions and thoughts, are indeed magnificent, divine creatures. An old adage I live by is: "If God wanted to hide, God would hide in human beings, because that's the last place we would think to look!" Also, there is either love or violence, and violence is a cry for love.

Stan Dale, *Author, Narrator, Speaker*

❧ THE KEY TO CONTENTMENT AND HAPPINESS ❦

PHOTO BY ROGER KURTNER

THE KEY TO CONTENTMENT AND HAPPINESS

Happiness is the perpetual possession of being well deceived.
Lionel Strachey

A happy man may be a successful bishop, dog catcher, movie actor or sausage monger, but no happy man ever produced a first-rate piece of painting, sculpture, music, or literature.
George Jean Nathan (1882-1958)

Happiness consists in the attainment of our desires, and in having only right desires.
Saint Augustine of Hippo (354-430)

The key to contentment is knowing where the keyhole is.
D. Gyllensvard, *Literary Staff Assistant*

The happiness habit is developed by simply practicing happy thinking. Make a mental list of happy thoughts and pass them through your mind several times every day. If an unhappiness thought should enter your mind, immediately stop, consciously eject it, and substitute a happiness thought. Every morning before arising, lie relaxed in bed and deliberately drop happy thoughts into your conscious mind. Let a series of pictures pass across your mind of each happy experience you expect to have during the day. Savor their joy. Such thoughts will help cause events to turn out that way.
Norman Vincent Peale, *from* THE POWER OF POSITIVE THINKING

The true test of happiness is whether you know what day of the week it is. A miserable man is aware of this even in his sleep. To be as cheerful and rosy-cheeked on Monday as on Saturday, and at breakfast as at dinner is to—well, make an ideal husband.
W.N.P. Barbellion (1889-1919)

THE KEY TO CONTENTMENT AND HAPPINESS

I believe that the key to contentment, fulfillment and happiness lies first in living up to the magnificent potential we were given at the moment we were conceived. When we ardently do the work we were meant to do, we no longer are laborers, we are creators.

My personal happiness has been to be a real help with the success of thousands of those who I have impacted thru my speaking and writing. What can compare with letters, faxes and phone calls from all over the world saying, "You inspired me." "You helped me."

I delight in the success of my friends, as my friend of the mind, Benjamin Franklin did. I also agree with my mental friend Rudyard Kipling who said, "Fill every minute with 60 seconds worth of distance run." I do my best to do this. Using all the seconds God gives me to create, help and love others is satisfying indeed.

My family is proud of me, as I am of them. I hope I have set an example for them to follow. When I realized that I would not be able to go to college, that my friends were leaving me, and that the two jobs I worked at to support my Mother were where I was stuck, I happened to be reading a biography of Amelia Earhart, the famous woman flyer. I heard her voice in the book. She told me, "Dottie, some of us have great runways already built for us. If you have one, TAKE OFF! But if you don't have one, then realize it is your job to grab a shovel and build a runway for yourself, and for those who will be coming behind you."

I thank God I grabbed that shovel.

Dottie Walters, *Motivational Speaker and Writer*

Happy are the rich, for they are never without means of consolation.

Countess Diane of Poitiers (1499-1566)

→ THE KEY TO CONTENTMENT AND HAPPINESS ←

An important key to lifelong happiness and contentment is learning how to deal with the difficult people with whom we all come into contact. There are lots of folks in the world who are simply mean, grouchy, nasty, argumentative, dishonest, rude, and self-centered. We can't avoid many of these bad individuals despite our best efforts because they are out in public, walking the streets, driving taxis and working in the stores where we shop. They are sometimes our bosses, co-workers, or employees. They might be our clients or customers. They may even be our close relatives who in a sadistic sort of way desire to be around us. Of course, the majority of people we interact with are pleasant enough but that small agitating minority can really ruin our day. We do have a choice in how we react in these conflict situations, and that can make all the difference.

Try to be attentive to those who are criticizing you, even if they are screaming. Just tell them that you are listening and they don't need to yell. Don't raise your voice. Keep calm and collected. Your opponent should soon cool off. As you hear them out, you may realize they have a legitimate complaint. If they do, assure them that you'll try to remedy the situation. If their gripe has no basis, as is usually the case for me personally, then briefly and calmly state your perception of the matter. Avoid as much possible the chance an argument. Tell them you are sorry that they feel the way they do. Try to understand how they may have gotten the wrong impression. Attempt to look at the matter from their side. If the person roasting you is wrong but happens to be your boss, tell them they are very perceptive and intelligent, that you really appreciate your job and you will do your best to never let it happen again—or something to that effect (be creative and try not to repeat yourself). Once the confrontation is over, whoever was involved, put it out of your mind. Don't hold a grudge or mull over it.

Forgive and forget. Remembering and replaying those nega-

THE KEY TO CONTENTMENT AND HAPPINESS

PHOTO BY MICHAEL SPOONEYBARGER

THE KEY TO CONTENTMENT AND HAPPINESS

tive thoughts will only create unhappiness and discontent.

There are various tricks or methods for dealing with disagreeable people:

1. Heap love and kindness on them, as difficult as that may be. Of course, anyone can like someone who is lovable. It is a special challenge to act positively towards one who is unlikable. Attempt to think good thoughts about them. Endeavor mentally to wish them the best even if you can't verbalize it to them directly. Others can read our body language easier than we might imagine, so it is important to have pleasant thoughts.

2. Try to figure out why they act the way they do. Make an effort to get to know them. Attempt to decipher their world view or thought patterns. Put yourself in their shoes. Once that person is understood, they usually become much easier to deal with.

3. Make it a game to see if you can make them smile or be happy. Almost everybody has something that they are fond of or like to talk about. As Joe Scruggs says, "Even trolls have moms." There is hardly anything more rewarding than to get a mean person to be nice, even if only for a brief period. Some nuts have really hard shells, but can be very enjoyable once they are cracked.

4. In a gentle and kind way, confront that person with their behavior. Explain what sort of decent, civil conduct you expect and appreciate. If you are too angry to talk, then write a carefully worded letter.

5. If all else fails—avoid them. Move and don't leave a forwarding address. Fake your death. Join the Federal Witness Protection Program and move to a small, nondescript town in the American Midwest.

J. Taylor Starkey

Happiness comes when you have just overcome a worrisome problem.

Dr. Joyce Brothers, *Author, Psychologist*

→ THE KEY TO CONTENTMENT AND HAPPINESS ←

I have heard it said that the first half of our lives we strive for success, the second half for significance. I am in the second half of my life and I am more convinced than ever that this is so.

I am seeking to move from a power figure to a wisdom figure. I have found happiness in investing my life in the lives of others. Christ said, "If you want to find your life then you will lose it." Lose it in service of Christ and others, and you discover what it is to really live.

I have been working now for 25 years taking athletes into prisons and conducting athletic clinics. Counselors then share with the inmates on a personal basis. I find my greatest joy and being of significance in helping these downtrodden and hated people of society, those that are incarcerated.

Bill Glass, *President, Bill Glass Ministries*

We have a lot to be thankful for. Our country is at peace. We have our health. We have the opportunity to make ourselves happy. Our country allows us the chance to go and do anything we can afford. It's our choice, if we have the courage, just to try and do it. Anything is possible as long as we believe it is possible and have faith—even happiness. But then again, what is happiness? Happiness is a state of mind, of well-being and contentment. This means we can be happy anytime, anywhere as long as we can accept where we are today and have faith in changing tomorrow.

The change in tomorrow has to be in us for we have the capability to think, work, influence and build friendships through Love because we are made in the image of God. The more friendships we have, the more contented and peaceful we are. By reaching out to others, we can make a difference in our happiness. A "smiling" attitude, even though difficult at times, makes our life worth living and exciting.

John Swoboda, *Engineer, Consultant*

➔ THE KEY TO CONTENTMENT AND HAPPINESS ◆

To live a fractional and flustered life, to feel pulled apart and at loose ends, to be all at odds with oneself, is to be unhappy. When, however, even temporarily life ceases to be thus discordant and becomes "a settled, strong and single wind, that blows one way," the experience is thrilling. To become completely absorbed in an exciting game, to lose oneself under the spell of great drama or music, to have a well-nigh perfectly focused hour of creativity as an artist or of fortunate eloquence as an orator, to find oneself in the thick of a conflict where the whole of oneself goes all out for the sake of a cause deeply believed in, even to forget oneself in the complete enjoyment of uncontrollable laughter—such occasions, when life ceases to be a fraction and becomes an integer, are profoundly satisfying. The basic urge of the human organism is toward wholeness. The primary command of our being is to get yourself together, and the fundamental sin is to be chaotic and unfocused.

While our very constitution urges us to get together, and makes happiness dependent on our doing so, life is continually pulling us apart. Wholeness involves facing constant inner conflicts between competing desires, accommodating potent emotional urges (such as sex, pugnacity, and selfishness) to the restrictions of society, and handling the lure of personal ideals and ambitions that collide with a dismaying sense of inadequacy. Difficult, however, though it is to save life from fragmentariness, the penalty for failure is terrific—a harassed, distracted life, drawn and quartered, that knows no serenity.

No disorganized personality can be put into any situation so fortunate that by itself it will make him happy, while a well-organized personality can confront with astonishingly satisfying results conditions that at first seem insurmountable.

Harry Emerson Fosdick, *from ON BEING A REAL PERSON **(1943)***

The poor man is happy; he expects no change for the worse.
Demetrius (First Century A.D.)

➔ THE KEY TO CONTENTMENT AND HAPPINESS ✦

PHOTO BY TAYLOR STARKEY

→ THE KEY TO CONTENTMENT AND HAPPINESS ←

A lifetime of happiness! No man alive could bear it; it would be hell on earth.

George Bernard Shaw (1856-1950)

The key to contentment is faith in God. It can't be acceptance by other people because you can never always please other people.

Jim Wright, *Former Speaker of the U.S. House of Representatives*

Pleasure is the only thing to live for. Nothing ages like happiness.

Oscar Wilde (1856-1900)

It's pretty hard to tell what does bring happiness; poverty and wealth have both failed.

Frank McKinney Hubbard (1868-1930)

I feel the key to contentment, fulfillment and happiness in life is attaining your goals. My success stemmed from the achievement of many small goals. As Governor, I am now in a position to make our state the best place it can be for our citizens.

Tommy G. Thompson, *Governor of Wisconsin*

Happiness for many is a matter of choice. While we can't control all of the events in our lives, in many cases we can control how we choose to react to those events. I tell people "It's Not What Happens To You, It's What You Do About It." To quote Albert Camus, "In the midst of winter I finally learned there was in me an invincible summer."

W. Mitchell, *Inspirational Speaker*

➔ THE KEY TO CONTENTMENT AND HAPPINESS ✦

> Happiness is a way station between too little and too much.
> **Channing Pollock (1880-1946),** *from Mr. Moneypenny*

"What is the key to contentment, fulfillment or happiness in life?" Obviously there is no simple single answer. Although I would like to reply by making the following introspective statements. I live by simple rules all of which center around concepts and aphorisms I learned as a child. First of all I strive everyday to make a contribution to the consciousness raising of us all. This is the foundation for all my goals. One way to help keep myself on course (contentment) is to work towards resolve everyday; that is, whenever I get into a problem area I try to resolve it as soon as possible so I won't have to carry around that emotional luggage for any extended period of time.

To appreciate what it takes to be fulfilled I refer to the following three steps I have identified for success: (1) Follow your heart; (2) Use your brain; (3) Work your rear end off.

And as to happiness, well, I strive to look for and respond to the Godness in all things, and the space between them. Happiness is what we receive from giving.

These uncomplicated precepts interwoven with a sense of humor, communication, cooperation and mutual respect built on a foundation of trust, make every day a rich tapestry of achievement, hope and love which is shared.

Tony Luna, *Speaker, Creativity and Business Instructor*

Our perception of events or actions that occur to us is strongly determined by our preexisting attitude. The emotion or state of mind that we possess usually dictates how we will respond to encounters, situations, or relationships. If we are angry and frustrated, then we will be agitated as we sit and wait for the red light to finally turn green. We will curse the other drivers in traffic as they impede our progress. If we are happy and content, we tend to drive with less haste, enjoy the weather, sing along with the radio, and wave at people we

THE KEY TO CONTENTMENT AND HAPPINESS

know. Our inner feelings dictate our actions. People and things become targets of our positive feelings or our negative feelings.

When people are sad and depressed they have no desire to get out—no wish to shop, visit or travel. They might reluctantly go to work but may make those around them unhappy or uncomfortable. A person who is clinically, medically depressed is the extreme example of this. If that person did get out, either by their own will or at someone else's insistence, and traveled to some fun destination or purchased some neat, new item, they still would not be content and happy. That depressed person might only be temporarily distracted from their melancholy mental state.

We must strive for a relatively stable, baseline mind set of contentment and happiness. This sometimes requires effort. Once this is achieved, the majority of our actions will result in positive pleasant experiences. In the sense of a cause and effect relationship, being happy is the cause. The effect is getting out, going on a fun trip, doing something for another in need, or enjoying work. That is to say, being happy and content results in the pleasurable performance of the actions. It is not the action that causes the positive emotion. Because we have made the decision to be happy and content, we will be able to experience the joy as the events occur. And if we are melancholy or self absorbed, that mind set will prevent or bar us from experiencing joy. Consciously determine that you will have a positive mental attitude and all else will follow.

J. Taylor Starkey

If you cannot be happy in one way, be in another; this facility of disposition wants but little aid from philosophy, for health and good humor are almost the whole affair. Many run about after felicity, like an absent-minded man hunting for his hat, while it is in his hand or on his head.

William Sharp (1855-1905)

THE KEY TO CONTENTMENT AND HAPPINESS

PHOTO BY FRANK TILLEY

THE KEY TO CONTENTMENT AND HAPPINESS

Just for today I will be happy. It is said that people will be as happy as they make up their minds to be. Happiness is from within; it is not a matter of externals.

Just for today I will try to adjust myself to what is, and not try to adjust everything to my own desires. I will take my family, my business, and my luck as they come and fit myself to them.

Just for today I will take care of my body. I will exercise it, care for it, nourish it, not abuse it nor neglect it, so that it will be a perfect machine for my bidding.

Just for today I will try to strengthen my mind. I will learn something useful. I will not be a mental loafer. I will read something that requires effort, thought and concentration.

Just for today I will exercise my soul in three ways. I will do somebody a good turn and not get found out. I will do at least two things I don't want to do, just for exercise.

Just for today I will be agreeable. I will look as well as I can, dress as becomingly as possible, talk low, act courteously, be liberal with praise, criticize not at all, nor find fault with anything and not try to regulate nor improve anyone.

Just for today I will try to live this day only, not to tackle my whole life problem at once. I can do things for twelve hours that would appall me if I had to keep them up for a lifetime.

Just for today I will have a program. I will write down what I expect to do every hour. I may not follow it exactly, but I will have it. I will eliminate two pests, hurry and indecision.

Just for today I will have a quiet half hour all by myself and relax. In this half hour sometimes I will think of God, so as to get a little more perspective into my life.

Just for today I will be unafraid, especially I will not be afraid to be happy, to enjoy what is beautiful, to love, and to believe that those I love, love me.

Sybil F. Partridge (Sister Mary Xavier),
Paraphrase from the poem "Just for Today"

THE KEY TO CONTENTMENT AND HAPPINESS

The key to contentment and happiness in life is appropriate medication!

This is a great truth for some individuals and a false hope for others. There are many who believe that a pill can cure the ills of life and so go through life seeking the proper blend of tranquilizers, antidepressants, or recreational drugs. A Xanax, Valium, or a few drinks can simply and effectively take the edge off, but that is a poor way to deal with stress. What may start as a short-term solution can become a life long bad habit. Escaping reality through intoxication from alcohol or illegal drugs may bring temporary pleasure but the euphoria never lasts.

Some people, on the other hand, genuinely need medication to live a normal life. Antidepressants can control real problems. These modern pharmaceuticals can have a dramatic, positive effect on particular individuals. Depression is not just a mood that people get in. It is an illness caused by a deficiency of a chemical in the brain called serotonin. The medications work by increasing the level of that chemical.

People who have depression have specific and recognizable symptoms. Most notable are a deep, overwhelming sadness and frequent crying for no major reason. Sleep disturbances are common in that the person may want to sleep all the time, or conversely they may have trouble falling asleep and then regularly wake up in the early morning hours and be unable to go back to sleep. Frustration, tension, or anxiety may be prominent. The person may develop a lack of desire to do formerly pleasurable activities, even to the point that they may resist even leaving their house. If one has these symptoms to a significant degree, they should seek medical help. Medication can have a miraculous effect and may be the only solution to the problem. Sometimes no amount of positive thought or stress relieving self-help methods will work.

There are times that people need professional help from psychologists, therapists, or counselors to overcome inappropriate reactions to stress. The pressures and disappointments of life impact everyone and must be dealt with. Through help, people can often change behaviors or thought patterns that are destructive to themselves or others. They can work through past negative experiences that rob them of joy in their present lives. Removal of these psychological barriers may be instrumental in achieving long-term happiness.

If you feel like counseling or medication could make a positive difference in your life then seek help. Sometimes you can't make it on your own. You may need a helping hand. Don't be afraid to ask.

J. Taylor Starkey, M.D.

This is the true joy of life: the being used for a purpose recognized by yourself as a mighty one; the being thoroughly worn out before you are thrown to the scrap-heap; the being a force of nature instead of a feverish, selfish clod of ailments and grievances.

George Bernard Shaw (1856-1950)

To look fearlessly upon life; to accept the laws of nature, not with meek resignation, but as her sons, who dare to search and question; to have peace and confidence within our souls—these are the beliefs that make for happiness.

Maurice Maeterlinck (1862-1949)

If this world affords true happiness, it is to be found in a home where love and confidence increase with the years, where the necessities of life come without severe strain, where luxuries enter only after their cost has been carefully considered.

A. Edward Newton (1863-1940)

Happiness is not the end of life; character is.

Henry Ward Beecher (1813-1887)

➤ THE KEY TO CONTENTMENT AND HAPPINESS ❈

PHOTO BY MYRA STARKEY

THE KEY TO CONTENTMENT AND HAPPINESS

The Greeks said grandly in their tragic phrase, "Let no one be called happy till his death;" to which I would add, "Let no one, till his death, be called unhappy."

Elizabeth Barrett Browning (1806-1861)

Real happiness is not dependent on external things. The pond is fed from within. The kind of happiness that stays with you is the happiness that springs from inward thoughts and emotions. You must cultivate your mind if you wish to achieve enduring happiness. You must furnish your mind with interesting thoughts and ideas. For an empty mind seeks pleasure as a substitute for happiness.

William Lyon Phelps (1865-1943)

The search for a single, inclusive good is doomed to failure. Such happiness as life is capable of, comes from the full participation of all our powers in the endeavor to wrest from each changing situation or experience its own full and unique meaning.

John Dewey (1859-1943)

Happy the man who, unknown to the world, lives content with himself in some retired nook! Whom the love of this nothing called Fame has never intoxicated with its vain smoke: who makes all his pleasure dependent on his liberty action, and gives an account of his leisure to no one but himself.

Nicolas Boileau-Despreaux (1636-1711)

The question, "What is the key to contentment, fulfillment or happiness in life?" is surely a provocative one for which I believe there is no simple answer. In four words I would say it would be—"Be True To Yourself."

Susan Ungaro, *Editor in Chief, Family Circle*

→ THE KEY TO CONTENTMENT AND HAPPINESS ←

The key to contentment is knowing how to enjoy what you have, and to be able to lose all desire for things beyond your reach.

Lin Yutang (1895-1976)

The true happiness is of a retired nature, and an enemy to pomp and noise; it arises, in the first place, from the enjoyment of one's self; and in the next, from the friendship and conversation of a few select companions; it loves shade and solitude, and naturally haunts groves and fountains, fields and meadows; in short, it feels everything it wants within itself, and receives no addition from multitudes of witnesses and spectators. On the contrary, false happiness loves to be in a crowd, and to draw the eyes of the world upon her. She does not receive satisfaction from the applause which she gives herself, but from the admiration which she raises in others. She flourishes on courts and palaces, theaters and assemblies, and has no existence but when she is looked upon.

Joseph Addison (1672-1719)

Egocentricity or self-centeredness can be one of the greatest barriers to contentment and happiness. Many people have this misconception that the world revolves around them. They have a poor understanding of the big picture and tend to view actions and events primarily from the standpoint of how they personally are affected. By nature, those who are egocentric will tend to be quite insensitive to the people around them. Discontent and unhappiness often come to that person when they don't get their way and to those around them whose lives they impact.

Egocentricity is a normal tendency. Any perceptive organism lower than man would almost exclusively view the world in that way. Since they can't think abstractly, it would be difficult for them to see things from any other perspective. Even those of our species seldom outgrow it before age three or four. As well adjusted adults we often get lazy, callous, or selfish and succumb to that attitude.

Egocentric individuals feel that their way of thinking or acting is the best way. They strongly desire that those who they view as significant agree with them. It stresses and irritates them immensely when others don't. They view other people from the perspective of how those individuals can serve their personal needs. They value them according to what they can do to further their self-serving agenda. They generally make plans without consulting the interested parties in the process, only seeking approval after their decisions have been made. Finding disagreement or resistance causes them anger and frustration. With much reluctance they may change their decisions but it often comes at such a high price to those who challenged them that they often are allowed to just have their way. It is usually the case that if they aren't happy, then nobody's going to be happy!

We are all occasionally guilty of self-centeredness or egocentricity. We get so deeply involved in some activity or so fully mentally engrossed in some idea or project that we lose sight of all else around us. This misconception is usually shattered when our personal world collides with the real world. We find that our thought or plan is not only relatively unimportant to others but that our excited description may elicit little more than a shrug of their shoulders or a polite, "that's interesting." We naturally would feel disappointment at their reaction but later might chuckle to ourselves for some of our grandiose ideas. On the other hand, if we get depressed or bitter at a lukewarm reception, we probably need to reassess the importance we are placing on ourselves or our schemes.

We are all important but generally no more important than each of our fellow men. All of our plans and ideas have merit but not at the expense or sacrifice of others. Excess self-love (narcissism) surely leads to frustration and unhappiness.

J. Taylor Starkey

➤ THE KEY TO CONTENTMENT AND HAPPINESS ⬅

PHOTO BY LAURA KASPAR

THE KEY TO CONTENTMENT AND HAPPINESS

As for a little more money and a little more time, why it's ten to one, if either one or the other would make you one whit happier. If you had more time, it would be sure to hang heavily. It is the working man who is the happy man. Man was made to be active, and he is never so happy as when he is so. It is the idle man who is the miserable man. What comes of holidays, and far too often of sight-seeing, but evil? Half the harm that happens is on these days. And, as for money—Don't you remember the old saying, "Enough is as good as a feast?" Money never made a man happy yet, nor will it. There is nothing in its nature to produce happiness. The more a man has, the more he wants. Instead of filling a vacuum, it makes one. If it satisfies one want, it doubles and trebles that want another way. That was a true proverb of the wise man, rely upon it: "Better is little with the fear of the Lord, than great treasure, and trouble therewith."

Benjamin Franklin (1706-1790)

Pain and suffering do not ennoble the human spirit. Pain and suffering breed meanness, bitterness, cruelty. It is only happiness that ennobles.

W. Somerset Maugham (1874-1965)

There is no record in history of a happy philosopher: they exist only in romantic legends.

H.L. Mencken (1880-1956)

Happiness is in the taste, and not in the things themselves. It is by having what we like that we are made happy, not by having what others think desirable.

Duc Francois de La Rochefoucauld (1613-1680)

THE KEY TO CONTENTMENT AND HAPPINESS

The key to contentment and happiness is to be united with God, through Christ, as the Spirit leads us through life's adventures.
Michael G. Maudlin, *Editor, Christianity Today*

Best trust the happy moments. What they give makes man less fearful of the certain grave and gives his work compassion and new eyes. The days that make us happy make us wise.
John Masefield (1878-1967)

The key to contentment is to follow the admonition of Christ—to love the Lord with all of our heart, soul and mind . . . and to love and serve others. Although we may fall short of this ideal, we should never stop trying to be better than we are.
Herbert H. Reynolds, *Chancellor of Baylor University*

To me, the key to a life of fulfillment and achievement is the statement which expresses my personal mission: "I will make the lives of others richer by the richness of my own."
Joe Batten, *Motivational Speaker, Author*

The key to contentment is having a couple of devoted dogs with understanding faces who will quietly listen to your problems without offering their own opinions or suggestions, who will accept praise without questioning your motives, and who will unconditionally greet you at the door with unbridled happiness when you return home.
J. Taylor Starkey

The habit of being happy enables one to be freed, or largely freed, from the domination of outward conditions.
Robert Louis Stevenson (1850-1894)

THE KEY TO CONTENTMENT AND HAPPINESS

Happiness can be built only on virtue, and must of necessity have truth for its foundation.

Samuel Taylor Coleridge (1772-1834)

Action may not always bring happiness; but there is no happiness without action.

Benjamin Disraeli (1804-1881)

The way I see it, if you want the rainbow, you gotta put up with the rain.

Dolly Parton

What is the key to contentment and happiness?
? ? ?

Buck Owens, *Singer, Songwriter*

Seek not happiness too greedily, and be not fearful of unhappiness.

Lao-tzu (b. 570 B.C.)

I earn what I eat, get what I wear, owe no man hate, envy no man's happiness, glad of other men's good, content with my harm.

William Shakespeare (1564-1616)

The key to contentment is doing what you like to do. I was in sales for over 20 years but I quit not too long ago because I got tired of the demanding customers. I adore my kids but I don't want them around all the time. I like to read, watch TV and work in the yard.

Mary B., *Age 74*

❧ THE KEY TO CONTENTMENT AND HAPPINESS ❦

PHOTO BY SUSIE MITCHEM

➔ THE KEY TO CONTENTMENT AND HAPPINESS ⭠

Contentment in life most certainly involves seeking after simplicity. An existence filled with endless activities, non-stop commitments and excessive material things to bother with is surely not satisfying. However, that lifestyle seems to be the norm in our society.

Our lives only slowly get complicated. This loss of simplicity doesn't occur over night. It may come through not being able to say no to a request to serve on another worthwhile committee or join another club. Or sometimes it's a new hobby or an additional project that edges into our already overburdened schedule. It may just be a slow increase or expansion of one's work load due to their success and competence, or perhaps more recently as a result of corporate downsizing. Maybe a once in a lifetime financial deal comes along that seems simply too good to pass up. Multiple kids may mean many multiple activities with constant running here and there to ensure their participation in all these supposedly necessary events. The older the children get, the more organizations and teams they join.

By examining our individual lives we could probably all make a list of ways to simplify, but here are some suggestions for starters:

1. Sell or rid yourself of some troubling investment or asset, even if you have to suffer a financial loss to do it. In the scheme of things, it probably won't be of great significance. It isn't worth the frequent worry, especially if it is something that bothers you while you are working, relaxing, or spending time with your family.

2. Give up some time consuming hobby that you don't really enjoy or that isn't worth the time or money that you are spending on it. Some people have old classic cars that seldom leave the garage, boats that are permanently parked under the shed, or collectibles and antiques that overflow from their shelves, closets and attic. Shopping for many individuals is an expensive hobby, if not an obsession, and

THE KEY TO CONTENTMENT AND HAPPINESS

seldom done out of necessity.

3. Clean out your closet. It can be a very cathartic or purifying experience. Give those old clothes away to charity. Someone can make good use of them. Fewer clothes and shoes will reduce your choices and so simplify your decision making each morning. You'll be surprised how out of style some of the stuff is and half of it is probably too small. When I cleaned out my closet I didn't find any moth damage but the shrink bugs had really wrecked havoc. I don't think I've gained a pound since college but all those old clothes I pulled out and tried on had shrunk tremendously. Shrink bugs are so tiny you can't see them but they've probably infested your closet too!

4. Quit the club, organization, or committee that you least enjoy attending. If you don't like going then you probably aren't making a meaningful contribution anyway and unless you are a really great actor, those whom you attend with likely realize you'd rather not be there.

5. Wear blue jeans more often and a suit and tie or formal clothes less frequently. Most people that you are around probably won't care and may even feel more relaxed around you. You'll definitely be more comfortable.

6. Sell, donate, or throw away things that you don't need that require your attention. It may be an old lawn mower or a machine that you were someday planning to repair. It might be broken down or unneeded future. It could be anything that is taking up space in your house, garage, or yard that needs work—and you often think about it—but just never get around to fixing.

7. Limit each of your children to one major activity and one minor activity. For instance, allow them to be part of a sports team that meets several times per week and then a group or club which meets only once a week. They'll be more relaxed and less fatigued. It will help them be focused and better at the things they do. They might welcome the new sim-

THE KEY TO CONTENTMENT AND HAPPINESS

plicity and less hectic lifestyle.

8. Decrease your standard of living. Pretend you are an industry or corporation—get efficient, reduce the non-essential, down-size, restructure. Move to a smaller house in a less pricey neighborhood. You'll have less maintenance and smaller note payments. Only buy cars that are several years old. Shop at discount stores more often. The heck with trying to keep up with the Joneses. Who cares what the neighbors think. If you end up spending a lot less, you can pay everything off and reduce the pressure to work so much.

Life will only be as complicated as we allow it to become. Simplification can reduce our worries and increase our contentment. It's our choice.

J. Taylor Starkey

There is this difference between happiness and wisdom; he that thinks himself the happiest man really is so; but he that thinks himself the wisest, is generally the greatest fool.

Charles Caleb Colton (1780-1832)

Happiness is neither within us only, or without us; it is the union of ourselves with God.

Blaise Pascal (1623-1662)

Surely happiness is reflective like the light of heaven; and every countenance, bright with smiles and glowing with innocent enjoyment, is a mirror, transmitting to others the rays of a supreme and evershining benevolence.

Washington Irving (1783-1859)

The foolish man seeks happiness in the distance, the wise grows it under his feet.

James Oppenheim (1882-1932)

❖ THE KEY TO CONTENTMENT AND HAPPINESS ❖

PHOTO BY TAYLOR STARKEY

→ THE KEY TO CONTENTMENT AND HAPPINESS ←

There is no one universal key to contentment and happiness. There are as many keys as there are people because each individual has his own personal definition of what constitutes this state of mind.

Perception is not a passive action. We add our own point of view to everything. This point of view is constructed by all we see, hear, touch, taste, or smell. Each and every experience is stored in our memory.

I believe that one cannot experience happiness unless he has experienced pain. These are the two sides of one coin.

Pain is the seed which produces the flower.
This flower of joy gives birth to the seed.
Inherent in each is a part of the other
And each the other doth need.
   Perception is the key we use
   To change everything into "real"
   We decide if it's a seed or flower.
   We decide what we wish to feel.
What's "out-there" is just raw material.
We create from this our life.
We choose happiness, peace and fulfillment
Or hate, anger and strife.

Lucy Gerald, *Devoted wife, 89 years young*

Happiness, after all, is an inner state of mind. It is little dependent on outside environment. Happiness has very little to do, for instance, with whether you are rich or not rich. Some of the most miserable persons I have come across in my life are rich people. It is true that poverty makes one miserable in a very acute way. But my point is that it is not wealth but coordination of one's thought and action which removes inner conflicts. It is in that way that integration of personality is achieved.

Jawaharlal Nehru (1889-1964)

→ THE KEY TO CONTENTMENT AND HAPPINESS ←

The search for contentment is a universal struggle for humans. Our late teenage and early adult years are a time when achievement and acquisition are emphasized. The thought is that if we just reach this goal or buy that thing, then we'll be happy and content. A person usually has a midlife crisis, or perhaps it should be called a contentment crisis, when this illusion of satisfaction through achievement finally ends, or at least begins its inevitable crumble.

We all progress through similar stages. As children we are happy to simply play. We want to please and be loved and accepted by our parents. As teenagers we are content if we can become independent individuals. That usually involves acting and dressing as much like our peers as possible. As young adults we seek fulfillment by obtaining the essential educational degrees and training to secure a great job. We look for the perfect spouse, get married, and then proceed to make that person into the perfect mate, whatever adjustments on their part are necessary. The next step is to start the family by having several intelligent, athletic, mentally well-balanced children, something that may be genetically or environmentally unlikely. During this time we may be so heavily involved in work with our free time consumed by church, civic, and recreational activities that we don't notice our kids growing up.

We continue down the path trod by a multitude of generations before us. By the mid-thirties to early forties, career advancement has occurred, the proper cars have been purchased, the necessary clubs and organizations joined, and a house befitting one's supposed position in life obtained. And then an uneasy feeling starts to creep over us. Contentment or fulfillment was vaguely promised to be at the end of this road.

We begin to question the journey. Where is the happiness that was guaranteed to be at this destination? It must be the wrong job, the wrong neighborhood or town, or the wrong spouse. So the foolish search for a new goal may begin.

If we are wise, we stop and realize that there is no set for-

THE KEY TO CONTENTMENT AND HAPPINESS

mula for contentment and happiness and that certainly position or possessions are not the answer. The recipe for fulfillment may be unique to each individual.

The old crusty cowboy Curly told burned-out Mitch (Billy Crystal) in City Slickers how city folks were all the same. They would spend 50 weeks a year getting knots in their rope and then think two weeks on a cattle drive would untie them all. "Do you know what the secret of life is?" Curly said. Mitch looked puzzled and replied he didn't. Curly held up his index finger and said, "It's just one thing . . . You stick to that and everything else doesn't mean nothin'."

"What's the one thing?" Mitch asked.

Curly wisely replied, "That's what YOU'VE got to figure out."

There is something that will make each one of us content and happy, but it isn't exactly the same for everybody. It is actually most likely a complex combination of factors including work, relationships, priorities, and perceptions. The answer will be a little different a year from now and maybe very different in 10 or 20 years. The secret can be found, only not possessed.

J. Taylor Starkey

Happiness is being married to your best friend.

Anonymous

The key to contentment and happiness is to have a sense of accomplishment—no matter how small. The world may be a better place because we are here. Respect by family and friends is important as is our enjoyment of the relationships with our children and grandchildren. Happiness also comes with faith in God.

Wayne Watkins, ***Engineer, Retired Corporate Executive***

➤ THE KEY TO CONTENTMENT AND HAPPINESS ❖

PHOTO BY JAMES WILCOX

THE KEY TO CONTENTMENT AND HAPPINESS

I believe happiness in one's life is attributed to keeping busy and doing positive and worthwhile activities. Doing for others and providing help in needed ways is the most rewarding feeling anyone can have. Your work becomes a pleasure and the feeling you receive is overwhelming when you are content in what you do. Happiness in most instances is self-made.

Gary Moses, *Teacher, Recreation Director*

There are as many nights as days, and the one is just as long as the other in the year's course. Even a happy life cannot be without a measure of darkness, and the word "happy" would lose its meaning if it were not balanced by sadness. It is far better to take things as they come along with patience and equanimity.

Carl Gustav Jung (1875-1961)

He who enjoys doing and enjoys what he has done is happy.

Johann Wolfgang Von Goethe (1749-1832)

God intends no man to live in this world without working; but it seems to me no less evident that He intends every man to be happy in this work.

John Ruskin (1819-1900)

Thank God every morning when you get up that you have something to do which must be done, whether you like it or not. Being forced to work, and forced to do your best, will breed in you temperance, self-control, and a hundred other virtues which the idle never know.

Charles Kingsley (1819-1875)

Happiness is the harvest of a quiet eye.

Austin O'Malley (1858-1932)

THE KEY TO CONTENTMENT AND HAPPINESS

One is happy as a result of one's own efforts, once he knows the necessary ingredients of happiness—simple tastes, a certain degree of courage, self-denial to a point, love of work, and above all, a clear conscience. Happiness is no vague dream, of that I now feel certain. By the proper use of experience and thought one can draw much from oneself, by determination and patience one can even restore one's health. So let us live life as it is, and not be ungrateful.
George Sand (1803-1876)

I think I could turn and live with animals, they are so placid and self-contained,
I stand and look at them long and long.
They do not sweat and whine about their condition,
They do not lie awake in the dark and weep for their sins,
They do not make me sick discussing their duty to God,
Not one is dissatisfied, not one is demented with the mania of owning things,
Not one kneels to another, nor to his kind that lived thousands of years ago,
Not one is respectable or unhappy over the whole earth.
Walt Whitman (1819-1892)

True contentment is the power of getting out of any situation all that there is in it.
G.K. Chesterton (1874-1936)

Contempt for happiness is usually contempt for other people's happiness, and is an elegant disguise for hatred of the human race.
If there were in the world today any large number of people who desired their own happiness more than they desired the unhappiness of others, we could have a paradise in a few years.
Bertrand Russell (1872-1970)

→ THE KEY TO CONTENTMENT AND HAPPINESS ←

Happiness, I have discovered, is nearly always a rebound from hard work. It is one of the follies of men to imagine that they can enjoy mere thought or emotion, or sentiment. One could as well try to eat beauty! For happiness must be tricked! She loves to see men at work. She loves sweat, weariness, self-sacrifice.

There is something fine in hard labor. One actually stops thinking. I often work long without any thought whatever, so far as I know, save that connected with the monotonous repetition of the labor itself—down with the spade, out with it, up with it, over with it—and repeat.

And yet sometimes—mostly in the forenoon when I am not at all tired—I will suddenly have a sense as of the world opening around me—a sense of its beauty and its meanings—giving me a peculiar deep happiness, that is near complete content.

David Grayson (1870-1946)

To find out what one is fitted to do and to secure an opportunity to do it is the key to happiness.

John Dewey (1859-1952)

The opposite of contentment is anxiety. And anxiety is a foreboding sense of the uncertainty of the future. It is the fear that develops as a result of feeling that we don't have everything under control. Anxiety creates tension and stress. Anxiety is a thief. It steals away our capacity to do, to achieve, and to enjoy the very things God has given us. As long as you feel anxious, you will not have peace. Anxiety by its very nature will breed self-centeredness. Trace the root cause of anxiety and you will find fear, unbelief, and our attempt to play God.

Charles Stanley, *Author, Baptist Minister*

❖ THE KEY TO CONTENTMENT AND HAPPINESS ❖

PHOTO BY TAYLOR STARKEY

➔ THE KEY TO CONTENTMENT AND HAPPINESS ❖

Discontent and frustration may come from constantly pushing ourselves and feeling like we must make the most of every minute. Some people are so driven that they can't seem to relax. It is as if they view idle time as a sin. One can only keep up such a pace for so long until they get burned out. Hard work and productivity is an important part of feeling content and fulfilled but our bodies and minds need rest too.

I once had a beautiful 20 acre piece of property in the country. It was a ridge of land that was covered with large oak trees and sloped down to a meadow that filled with Texas wildflowers each spring. Below that was a rocky creek bed with a clear stream that meandered through it. It was an enjoyable place to picnic, hike, and swim. I spent many weekend days there clearing brush, piling it up, and then lighting bonfires. Sometimes I would roast marshmallows and weenies over a campfire with the kids. On clear nights, we would look with awe at the bright stars as they can only be seen in a dark country sky away from the city lights. I taught my oldest son, Miles, how to shoot a pistol out there. We had some good times exploring and looking for deer and interesting plants.

My problem was that I was younger and more foolish then and did not know how to relax. I could not leave my intensity, focus and compulsive behavior from my medical clinic behind. If a big limb had fallen, I felt the need to chainsaw it into useful firewood, stack that neatly, and then burn the smaller branches. I was compelled to hack down every little thorn bush that would spring up and spray copious amount of weed killer on every poison ivy plant on the property. I searched for ant mounds to poison. I trimmed trees and blazed new roads and trails through the brush. Perhaps I was unconsciously trying to recreate the Garden of Eden.

I finally got tired of going out there and working so hard. It seemed that I could not just sit, relax, unwind and simply enjoy nature. I felt I had to control it. I put it on the market. It naturally sold quickly since it was so meticulously maintained.

THE KEY TO CONTENTMENT AND HAPPINESS

I just didn't want to own it anymore—too much trouble. I thought to myself, "What difference will it make a thousand years from now if I clear off all that property?"

The truth is . . . what difference will anything that we do make a thousand years from now? Can you recall any personally meaningful events that occurred about 1000 A.D.? Do you know who the powerful emperor of Mighty China was then? Who was the wealthiest man in all of Europe? These things were very important then but they matter very little now. Many mighty ancient cities lay buried under the sand.

Don't feel like you must constantly be achieving some new goal. Take time to relax and enjoy life now. Spend some lazy hours with your wife and kids. Take your watch off and go float in an inner tube down a slow river. Explore the countryside and don't think about real estate prices. Smell flowers without picking them. Enjoy the view without trying to take the perfect picture. Go shopping with nothing on your list. Play golf and don't keep score . . . and if you don't like the shot you make, hit another ball.

There is one very important thing to remember when you are relaxing—and that is to RELAX! Quit striving for perfection in your time of recreation. Just have fun. Find a child and take them with you. They usually still remember how to play. Save your intensity and concentration for work.

J. Taylor Starkey

In order that people may be happy in their work, these three things are needed: They must be fit for it; they must not do too much of it; and they must have a sense of success in it.

John Ruskin (1819-1900)

No medicine can cure what happiness cannot.

Gabriel Garcia Marquez, *from Of Love and Other Demons*

THE KEY TO CONTENTMENT AND HAPPINESS

The key to contentment and happiness is to know that which in life can be changed for the better, that which cannot, and realizing the difference. It is important to be able to accept pain as a part of existence, and not an enemy. The acquisition of happiness is not possible. We can only pursue a full life and happiness will ensue. In the midst of unhappiness and tragedy there can be joy. When Victor Frankl was in the German concentration camp, he had everything taken away from him . . . everything except his ability to decide how he would react to the things that impacted him. We choose too. As Nietzsche said, "To live is to suffer, to survive is to understand the meaning of the suffering."

Bill Dugat, *Episcopal minister*

Human happiness seems to consist in three ingredients: action, pleasure, and indolence. And though these ingredients ought to be mixed in different proportions, according to the disposition of the person, yet no one ingredient can be entirely wanting without destroying in some measure the relish of the whole composition.

David Hume (1711-1776)

The key to contentment is living your passion. Do what you know to be what you love and not what anyone else says you should do. And hang around people who love to support, nurture, and empower your greatness.

Helice Bridges, *Speaker, Author, Corporate Trainer*

In vain do they talk of happiness who never subdued an impulse in obedience to a principle. He who never sacrificed a present good to a future good, or a personal to a general one, can speak of happiness only as the blind do of colors.

Horace Mann (1796-1859)

THE KEY TO CONTENTMENT AND HAPPINESS

PHOTO BY HERBERT DOUD

➔ THE KEY TO CONTENTMENT AND HAPPINESS ✦

Happiness, like every other emotional state, has blindness and insensibility to opposing facts given it as its instinctive weapon for self-protection against disturbance.

William James (1842-1910)

Do not speak of your own happiness to one less fortunate than yourself.

Plutarch (46-120 A.D.)

The key to contentment and happiness first and primarily is a deep faith in Jesus Christ. This necessitates daily commitment to studying the Bible, being a servant to others, and most importantly, time in prayer.

Relationships with others are extremely important, most especially immediate family including your spouse, children and grandchildren.

It is important to set goals in life that are a challenge, yet are attainable. Don't be afraid to try new opportunities that come along in life, even if it means stepping out into the unknown.

Rex Kirkley, *Semi-retired Family Doctor, Grandfather, Fisherman*

The keys to my contentment and happiness are my children. Watching my children grow, helping them to learn and sharing their experiences has added dimension to my life. Children are highly perceptive and yet, innocent. They appreciate nature's simple pleasures—and through them I share their joy of discovery. My children have enriched and fulfilled my life bringing me a heightened sense of contentment and happiness.

Bob Miller, *Governor of Nevada*

THE KEY TO CONTENTMENT AND HAPPINESS

The manner of a man's life is a clue to what he on reflection regards as happiness. Persons of low taste (always in the majority) hold that it is pleasure. Accordingly they ask for nothing better than the sort of life which consists of having a good time. The utter vulgarity of the herd of men comes out in their preference for the sort of existence a cow leads. The gentleman however, identifies happiness with honor. Again, why do men seek honor? Surely in order to confirm the favorable opinion they have formed of themselves. They want to be honored for their moral qualities.

Happiness is an end, and not the means to an end. It is the final good. We choose it for its own sake and not for the sake of achieving something higher. Happiness has a high degree of finality.

Happiness cannot be achieved in less than a complete lifetime. One swallow does not make a summer; neither does one fine day. And one day, or indeed any brief period of felicity, does not make a man entirely and perfectly happy.

You cannot quite regard a man as happy if he be ugly to look at, or of humble origin, or alone in the world and childless, or—what is probably worse—with children or friends who have not a single good quality.

Happiness is an activity of the soul in conformity with perfect goodness and virtue. Perfect goodness is the performance of our individual functions in life with excellence. Virtue is a confirmed disposition to act rightly, the disposition being itself formed by a continuous series of right actions.

Aristotle (384-322 B.C.)

The key to contentment and happiness is to align your thoughts, words, and actions with those of God, to the best of your ability.

Jeep Collins, *Jewelry Maker*

→ THE KEY TO CONTENTMENT AND HAPPINESS ←

One of our greatest joys in life should be the time we spend with our spouse and children. Good relationships in these areas can make or break us in regards to our sense of contentment and fulfillment. On the questionnaire I sent out regarding "the key to contentment and happiness," many of those responding indicated the important role that their intimate family played. Although some may have hastily given that answer thinking that it was simply the right response, I'm certain that for many the reply was heart-felt.

A married person's spouse should really be their best friend. No human, neither friend nor family should rank higher in their eyes. They should be most esteemed and their companionship and opinions of greatest importance. I suspect that one might think I am exaggerating but if these things are not true in a marriage then it probably leaves much to be desired. That union only works with total commitment and devotion. Anything less results in a breakdown of the marital relationship.

It is almost a miracle that our mates still love us despite the things we say or do sometimes, particularly when we are fatigued, self-absorbed, rushed, or angry and have our guard down. At times our "true feelings" are probably better left unsaid. Others may really think we have our act together but our partner may know better. The forgiveness that comes with total love allows marriages to function and survive. With love we can grow old and wrinkled together.

The importance of our children cannot be underemphasized. They can be the greatest joy OR the biggest heartache of our lives. Children must be raised well. They are born with different and unique personalities as anyone who has more that one offspring can attest. But as sweet and loving as little kids may be, they are all uncivilized and self-centered in their natural state. Left to their own desires they would grow into selfish, demanding, insensitive adolescents and adults—so they must be disciplined and trained to avert such disastrous re-

❧ THE KEY TO CONTENTMENT AND HAPPINESS ❦

PHOTO BY L'NELL STARKEY

THE KEY TO CONTENTMENT AND HAPPINESS

sults. Kids can be highly resistant to this and may make your life miserable when you attempt to alter their ways. But it must be done for everyone's future happiness.

Children are not just miniature versions of adults. They think differently than us. Kids are trusting and innocent—they give love with no other desire than attention. Adults are suspicious and worldly—they often show affection with desires for secondary gain. Children go out of their way to step in mud, water puddles, or piles of leaves. We detour to avoid messing up our shoes. Kids need to be able to act like carefree kids. Raising children is not a contest where we race other parents to see whose kids can read, speak French, and play the piano first. It doesn't matter if you child is better than theirs in basketball or football. Each kid should be encouraged to be productive, do their best, and live up to their potential but they should not be compared to other children anymore than we should compare our spouse to the mates of others.

In raising children we must provide strong direction. In today's society I fear that we go too far in respecting or condoning the poorly thought out, immature beliefs and actions of children. We will go to great lengths to compromise and avoid conflict. I don't remember it being that way when I grew up. We should stand firm on the really important moral issues. There are lesser issues that allow flexibility and experimentation in decision making. As parents we must individually decide which are which. And as kids age and show maturity in their judgments, they must be allowed to make more of their own choices. Past age 18 they begin to resent unsolicited advice or direction and we can only be ready to offer help when they ask. The time to shape them is generally well before their mid-teenage years.

When we get off work we must not come home with the same attitude of maximizing the efficient use of time. Kids don't like strict time schedules for fun and recreation (and neither do most adults). It is impossible to force a good time.

THE KEY TO CONTENTMENT AND HAPPINESS

A brief amount of "quality" time is no substitute for quantity of time. You can never foretell when those special moments or memorable conversations will occur.

In the end, it won't really matter what sort of cars we owned, houses we lived in or important jobs we had. Those things all fade away. Our final and best joys will be our happy, well-adjusted children and grand kids who truly want to come visit us and share our memories AND that old wrinkled friend who will still sit by your side and hold your hand.

J. Taylor Starkey

The haunts of happiness are varied, but I have more often found her among little children, home firesides, and country houses than anywhere else.

Sydney Smith (1771-1845)

The key to happiness is family, church, achieving personal goals, and last but not least, hunting and fishing.

E. Benjamin Nelson, *Governor of Nebraska*

I accept life unconditionally. Most people ask for happiness on condition. Happiness can only be felt if you don't set any condition.

Arthur Rubinstein (1887-1982)

The key to contentment and happiness would be having your compulsive husband learn to type his own writings and particularly his everchanging manuscripts.

Myra Starkey, *Wife of Author*

The Key to Contentment and Happiness Is . . .

To truly know God and to discover His will for you and then to carry out that special mission;

To not overemphasize your transient importance or place on Earth;

To realize early in life the folly of egocentricity;

To appreciate that variety is the spice of life but that honest, productive, diligent labor is the meat and potatoes;

To value relationships more than gold and to never knowingly breach or violate the trust of another human being;

To understand that you can be a powerful positive or negative influence in the lives of others, that you can make a difference, that only serving others and not self can give lasting fulfillment.

J. Taylor Starkey

What is the Key to Contentment and Happiness?

After reading this book, perhaps you have a better idea as to what you think the key to contentment and happiness is. Write it down. Sign your name and date it. Share it with a friend. If you can remember to do it, pull this book off the shelf in a few years, dust it off, and read again what you wrote.

For me, the key to contentment and happiness is . . .

I would like to hear from you if you have comments, stories, quotes, questions or want to share your thoughts. If you don't want it published, make sure you tell me.
J. Taylor Starkey M.D.,
404 West Guadalupe Street,
Victoria, Texas 77901

Addresses of Selected Contributors

Joe Batten
Joe Batten Associates, 4505 S.W. 26th Street, Des Moines, IA 50321

Harold Bloomfield, M.D.
1110 Luneta Drive, Del Mar, CA 92014

Helice Bridges
Difference Makers International, Helice Bridges Communications, P.O. Box 2115, Del Mar, CA 92014

Mike Buettell
307 Grand Canal, Balboa Island, CA 92662

Jack Canfield
President, Self-Esteem Seminars, 6035 Bristol Parkway, Culver City, CA 90230

Stan Dale
President, Human Awareness Institute, 1720 S. Amphlett Blvd., Ste. 128, San Mateo, CA 94402

Burt Dubin
President, Personal Achievement Institute, 1 Speaking Success Road, Kingman, AZ 86402-6543

Bobbie Gee
Bobbie Gee Enterprises, 1540 S. Coast Highway, Suite 206, Laguna Beach, CA 92651

Bill Glass
Bill Glass Ministries, P.O. Box 9000, Cedar Hill, TX 75104-9000

Mark Victor Hansen
Hansen and Associates, P.O. Box 7665, Newport Beach, CA 92658-7665

D. Trinidad Hunt
Elan Enterprises, 47-430 Hui Nene St., Kaneohe, HI 96744

Florence Littauer
President, CLASS Speakers, 1645 S. Rancho Sante Fe Road, Suite 102, San Marcos, CA 92069

Patricia Lorenz
7457 S. Pennsylvania, Oak Creek, WI 53154

Tony Luna
Tony Luna Creative Services, 819 North Bel Aire Drive, Burbank, CA 91501-1205

Glen McIntyre
McIntyre and Associates, 6349 Via Cozumel, Camarillo, CA 93012

W. Mitchell, C.P.A.E.
12014 W. 54th Drive #100, Arvada, CO 80002

Dottie Walters
Box 1120, Glendora, CA 91740

Bettie B. Youngs, Ph.D.
3060 Racetrack View Drive, Del Mar, CA 92014

Acknowledgments
and Thanks to:

Dr. Charles Stanley, IN TOUCH MINISTRIES, P.O. Box 7900, Atlanta Georgia for quotes from "The Key to Contentment."

Thomas Merton, *No Man Is An Island,* copyright 1955, The Abbey of Our Lady of Gethsemani, Harcourt Brace Jovanovich, Publishers.

Dale Carnegie's Scrapbook, copyright 1959, Dale Carnegie and Associates.

Norman Vincent Peale, *The Power of Positive Thinking,* copyright 1952, 1987 Prentice Hall-Simon and Schuster.

Harry Emerson Fosdick, *On Being a Real Person,* copyright 1943, Harper and Brothers.

Stephen Covey, *The Seven Habits of Highly Effective People,* copyright 1989, Stephen R. Covey, Simon and Schuster.

The Living Bible, Copyright 1971, Tyndale House Publishers.

. . . and finally, to Becky Moore for her help in the initial typing, and to Jim and Barbara Burke and Andrea Pinc for their professional creative assistance.

Index of Authors

A
Abd-er Rahman III 45
Addison, Joseph 7, 13, 21, 96
Allen, George 72
Allen, Tim 43
Almond, Lincoln 16
Anderson, Eric, M.D. 9
Anonymous 4, 5, 11, 19, 28, 29, 35, 36, 51, 109
Archbold, Ralph 5
Aristotle 120
Ash, Mary Kay 44
Ashcroft, John 63
Augustine of Hippo (Saint) 79
Aurelius, Marcus 19

B
B., Mary 101
Balzac, Honore de 55
Barbellion, W.N.P. 79
Barnhart, David 55
Barrie, Sir James M. 55
Barry, Dave 59
Barry, Marion Jr. 53
Bartley, Robert 51
Batten, Joe 100
Beecher, Henry Ward 44, 93
Bennett, Arnold 53
Bickerstaffe, Isaac 75
Bloomfield, Harold H., M.D. 48
Boileau-Despreaux, Nicolas 95
Bolin, Dan 35
Bridges, Helice 117
Brothers, Dr. Joyce 83
Browning, Elizabeth Barrett 95
Brown, Helen Gurley 3
Bruyere, Jean de La 35
Buettell, Mike 45

Burns, George 3
Burton, Ben 20
Bush, George W. 33
Byron, Lord (George Gordon) 9

C
Canfield, Jack 47
Carl Gustav 111
Carnegie, Dale 8, 64, 67
Carper, Thomas R. 49
Chekhov, Anton 28
Chesterton, G.K. 112
Clark, Dan 4
Cohen, Alan 16
Coleman, Melba 13
Coleridge, Samuel Taylor 101
Collins, Jeep 120
Colton, Charles Caleb 105
Cousins, Norman 11
Covey, Stephen 72
Cowper, William 59

D
Dale, Stan 77
Davis, David E. Jr. 73
Demetrius 85
Dewey, John 95, 113
Diane of Poitiers (Countess) 80
Disraeli, Benjamin 101
Dubin, Burt 29
Dugat, Bill 117
Duncan, Gaylan 49
Durant, Will 19
Dyer, Wayne 45

E
Edwards, Edwin W. 27
Eisenhower, Dwight D. 60

Epictetus 3, 5
Epicurus 25
Esar, Evan 33

F
Farrar, Steve 35
Fichte, Immanuel Hermann (von) 75
Fontenelle, Bernard 39
Fordice, Kirk 43
Fosdick, Harry Emerson 85
Franklin, Benjamin 65, 99
Fripp, Patricia 59
Frost, Robert 75
Fuller, Thomas 13, 16, 49
Fults, Timothy 59

G
Gay, John 7
Gee, Bobbie 75
Gelinas, Rick 21
Gerald, Lucy 107
Glass, Bill 84
Goethe, Johann Wolfgang Von 111
Goldsmith, Oliver 64
Gonzalez, Henry B. 15
Gracian, Baltasar 28
Gramm, Phil 19
Grassley, Chuck 21
Grayson, David 113
Griffin, Glenn C., M.D. 40
Gump, Forrest (Winston Groom) 51
Gyllensvard, D. 79

H
Hance, Joseph, M.D. 17
Hansen, Mark Victor 55
Hazlitt, William 48
Hendricks, Howard G. 49
Hoffer, Eric 3
Hubbard, Frank McKinney 87
Hubbard, L. Ron 67
Humboldt, Wilhelm (Von) 56
Hume, David 117
Hunt, D. Trinidad 44

I
Irving, Washington 105

J
James, William 119
Jefferson, Thomas 37
Jesus Christ 40
Jewish Folk Tale 17
Johnson, Samuel 19, 28, 39, 48

Jones, Brereton C. 75
Judd, Naomi 64

K
Keating, Frank 37
Keller, Helen 60
Kerrey, J. Robert 56
Kingsley, Charles 111
Kirkley, Rex 119
Kushner, Rabbi Harold 5

L
Landry, Tom 64
Langbridge, Frederick 43
Lao-tzu 101
Leach, Robin 5
Lewis, C.S. 27
Lincoln, Abraham 8
Linkletter, Art 7
Littauer, Florence 43
Locke, John 35
Longfellow, Henry Wadsworth 9
Lorenz, Patricia 37
Lowell, James Russell 29
Luna, Tony 88

M
MacDonald, George 59
Maeterlinck, Maurice 93
Mann, Horace 117
Mannering, Dennis 35
Marano, Hara Estroff 57
Marquez, Gabriel Garcia 116
Marx, Karl 21
Mary Xavier (Sister), *See Partridge, Sybil F.*
Masefield, John 100
Matthews, Russ 67
Maudlin, Michael G. 100
Maugham, W. Somerset 99
May, Rollo 29
McCarty, Hanoch 60
McIntyre, Glen 9
Mencken, H.L. 21, 99
Merton, Thomas 36
Mill, John Stuart 68
Miller, Bob 119
Milton, John 65
Mitchell, W. 87
Moses, Gary 111
Mother Goose 56
Murphy, Dr. Michael J. 27
Myra, Harold 53

N
Nathan, George Jean 63, 79
Nehru, Jawaharlal 107
Nelson, E. Benjamin 124
Newton, A. Edward 93
North, Oliver 56

O
Olesen, Erik 9
O'Malley, Austin 111
Oppenheim, James 105
O'Sullivan, John 63
Ovid 29
Owens, Buck 101

P
Parton, Dolly 101
Partridge, Sybil F. (Sister Mary Xavier) 91
Pascal, Blaise 105
Peale, Norman Vincent 72, 79
Phelps, William Lyon 48, 95
Plutarch 119
Pollock, Channing 88
Povich, Maury 60

Q
Qubein, Dr. Nido 15

R
Rangel, Charles 33
Raspberry, William 27
Rather, Dan 56
Reasoner, Robert W. 59
Renshaw, Tom M.D. 16
Reynolds, Herbert H. 100
Robertson, Pat 39
Rochefoucauld, Duc Francois de La 48, 65, 99
Rohn, Jim 16
Rousseau, Jean Jacques 45
Rubinstein, Arthur 124
Russell, Bertrand 33, 60, 112
Ruskin, John 67, 111, 116

S
Salsbury, Glenna 23
Sand, George 35, 64, 112
Santayana, George 25
Scruggs, Joe 51
Seneca, Lucius 25, 36
Shakespeare, William 101
Sharp, William 89
Shaw, George Bernard 4, 21, 59, 87, 93
Shilanski, Floyd 8
Smith, Logan Pearsall 39
Smith, Sydney 124
Solomon (King) 37
Spurgeon, Charles Haddon 13
Stanley, Charles 113
Starkey, J. Taylor 11, 20, 23, 31, 41, 52, 61, 65, 69, 76, 81, 88, 92, 96, 100, 103, 105, 115, 121, 125
Starkey, Myra 124
Steen, Sharon 47
Stevenson, Robert Louis 100
Stoppard, Tom 28
Strachey, Lionel 79
Swift, Johnathan 5
Swindoll, Chuck 11
Swoboda, John 84

T
Thatcher, Margaret 55
Thomas, Craig 44
Thompson, Tommy G. 87

U
Ungaro, Susan 95

W
Walters, Dottie 80
Watkins, Wayne 109
Waxman, Henry A. 44
West, Dr. Ross 8
White, Vanna 4
Whitman, Walt 13, 112
Wilcox, Ella Wheeler 37
Wilde, Oscar 36, 45, 55, 87
Williams, Sandra S. 51
Winget, Larry 29
Wotton, Sir Henry 4
Wright, Jim 87

Y
Young, Edward 9
Youngs, Bettie B. 3
Yutang, Lin 13, 51, 96

Z
Zellmer, Daniel 15